Having had the pleasure to work with Peter and his team in the past, I learned firsthand the importance of process, performance, and people. I'm excited to now have that knowledge and guidance as a tool to pull out whenever needed in *Results, Not Reports*.

LEN WOLIN

Senior Vice President of Hotel Operations, Sonesta International Hotels Corporation

Leading an organization in turbulent and changing times is difficult. *Results, Not Reports* will become an outstanding and trusted reference for performance improvement. This book is very useful for any leader or manager.

MARCO CALABRETTA-DUVAL

President, Pattison Sign Group

Peter Follows provides a commonsense look into sustainable change management. *Results, Not Reports* helps leaders maneuver through a myriad of known improvement concepts and organize them into a comprehensive map toward a culture of performance.

JEAN FILION

Chief Executive Officer and Président et Chef de la Direction, Nellson LLC

Having experienced the consulting services of Peter Follows and his team working directly within our organization, *Results, Not Reports* is not just a title; it is a reality. Our company saw significant positive change from their hands-on approach. They implement change rather than recommend change. This is a must-read for leaders looking to effect positive productivity improvement while maintaining and likely improving customer service.

DAVE JOHNSTON
Former President and Chief Operating Officer, Canada, Great-West Life Assurance Company

Leading an organization through change that will maximize bottom-line impact is difficult in any environment. *Results, Not Reports* is a refreshingly clear guide on how to do it well. This is a valuable tool for any leader or manager looking to achieve and maintain results-oriented change.

GREG SECORD
Former President of ADP Canada and Comdata North America Trucking

Results, Not Reports is a must-read for senior leaders who want specific, useable, and proven guidance for sustaining operational excellence in today's rapidly changing environment. Peter Follows's easy-to-use road map works as well for leaders of early-stage start-ups as it does for storied, mature organizations. His principles guide all leaders in effecting the mindset and process changes required for long-term success.

CHRISTINA JENKINS, MD
Venture Partner, PVP

Peter Follows gives us a guided tour for creating a high-performance organization. This eye-opening, commonsense, and engaging read weaves the perfect balance of new ways of thinking and practical experience.

THOMAS HOGAN

Cofounder and Chief Financial Officer, Areté Collective

Results, Not Reports is an indispensable guide for any business leader seeking to sustainably improve organizational performance. Peter's practical insights and real-world examples provide actionable strategies that can drive meaningful results for organizations of all sizes and industries.

BRUCE HODGES

Former CEO, ING Insurance, Malaysia

Peter Follows provides a concise and practical blueprint for performance improvement at all levels of any organization. *Results, Not Reports* is a powerful reference guide for any manager and CEO alike.

TONY PUCILLO

Partner, Corinthian Capital Group

With *Results Not Reports*, Peter Follows offers leaders an essential and heartfelt guide to performance improvement. You'll likely see your own organization in some of these pages.

ANDREW BRENTON

CEO, Turtle Creek Asset Management, Inc.

Results, Not Reports is an essential guide to performance excellence for CEOs and frontline managers alike. Peter Follows, one of the foremost change and transformation leaders of our time, provides a practical, evidence-based approach to achieving desired performance results while sharing real-life experiences and insights from his work in nearly every industry, from hospitality and healthcare to manufacturing and financial services, just to name a few.

MICHAEL J. ZACCAGNINO
President, Fund Love/Lucania Partners

Results, Not Reports provides practical insights for delivering meaningful changes to any business. Peter Follows leverages his years of hands-on experience to provide a pragmatic roadmap for any leader seeking sustainable improvements and results for their organization.

DAVE ARNOLD
General Manager and Chief Operating Officer, Golden State Medical Supply

RESULTS

NOT REPORTS

PETER FOLLOWS

NOT REPORTS

BUILDING **EXCEPTIONAL**

ORGANIZATIONS

BY INTEGRATING **PROCESS,**

PERFORMANCE, AND **PEOPLE**

Forbes | Books

Published by Forbes Books, Charleston, South Carolina.
An imprint of Advantage Media Group.

Forbes Books is a registered trademark, and the Forbes Books colophon is a trademark of Forbes Media, LLC.

Printed in the United States of America.

10 9 8 7 6 5 4 3 2 1

ISBN: 979-8-88750-050-8 (Hardcover)
ISBN: 979-8-88750-051-5 (eBook)

LCCN: 2023907414

Cover design by Matthew Morse.
Layout design by Megan Elger.

This custom publication is intended to provide accurate information and the opinions of the author in regard to the subject matter covered. It is sold with the understanding that the publisher, Forbes Books, is not engaged in rendering legal, financial, or professional services of any kind. If legal advice or other expert assistance is required, the reader is advised to seek the services of a competent professional.

Since 1917, Forbes has remained steadfast in its mission to serve as the defining voice of entrepreneurial capitalism. Forbes Books, launched in 2016 through a partnership with Advantage Media, furthers that aim by helping business and thought leaders bring their stories, passion, and knowledge to the forefront in custom books. Opinions expressed by Forbes Books authors are their own. To be considered for publication, please visit **books.Forbes.com**.

To all the clients, mentors, and colleagues at Carpedia, whose insights and efforts brought life to an aspiration from many years ago.

CONTENTS

WHY CHANGE
REQUIRES CHANGE

*We cannot solve our problems with the same
thinking we used when we created them.*
—ALBERT EINSTEIN

One of my earliest consulting projects was at a four-star hotel. The winter Olympics were being held in Calgary, which was unusually warm that year, and the city was bustling with energy and excitement. Two of my former teammates were playing for the US Olympic hockey team. They set me up with box seats for every game.

Unfortunately, two weeks before the games were slated to start, the hotel company decided that doing the project concurrently would be too distracting, so the project was put on hold. As a result, I got transferred to another project, which happened to be at a potash mine in the middle of nowhere. It was the first time I'd experienced a cold so bone-chilling you had to plug in your car each night so that the battery didn't freeze.

As disappointed as I was, what I didn't know at the time was that the next six months would forever change my perspective. I learned how it's possible to examine a business operation—any business operation—with the right tools and a growth mindset and to find ways to improve it.

I was assigned to the mining production area. I had the good fortune to be introduced to a gentleman named Leroy who was the mine manager and a veritable mountain of a man. I shook his oversized hand, and he looked at me, chuckled, and said, "What the hell are you going to teach me about running a mine?" Because I was young and inexperienced, I was thinking the same thing.

Leroy knew every inch of the mine. He understood better than the maintenance engineers how the mining equipment worked. He knew more than company geologists about the advantages and disadvantages of working in a soft rock mine. Anytime Leroy spoke, the other workers stopped what they were doing and paid close attention to his advice.

> It's possible to examine a business operation—any business operation— with the right tools and a growth mindset and to find ways to improve it.

But he hadn't really thought about how the mine operated in a very long time. He had become something of a caretaker of the way they always did things, and he'd stopped questioning why. So as irritating as it may have been at first, he eventually grew accustomed to me tagging along asking questions all day.

Potash, incidentally, is an ore that is mined to make fertilizer. This mine was quite deep. You got to it by going straight down a mine shaft that was roughly twice the height of the Empire State Building.

The mining operation itself was effectively digging rows of underground tunnels that didn't go anywhere. These were called rooms. There was a limit to how long the rooms could be because the tunnel would eventually collapse onto itself due to the soft rock environment and the gradual shifting of the ore deposit.

Because of this gradual shifting of sediment, it was surprisingly warm deep in the mines, despite it being bitingly cold at the surface. The massive boring machines dug out the rock, which fell onto conveyors that eventually made their way up to a processing mill. The basic process was to add conveyors as you moved along and then reclaim the equipment as you retreated.

All the miners knew how to lay down the conveyors, and they knew how to reclaim them. Some were also skilled in running the boring machines. Leroy and I spent a great deal of time observing how the different shifts operated through all stages of the process.

Despite the repetitive nature of the operation, challenges arose, as they always do. The boring machines occasionally broke down, the conveying equipment got damaged, and the conveyor system itself was prone to mismatched capacities, which caused unscheduled delays.

There was also no defined process for advancing or reclaiming. The equipment itself had been innovated and improved over the years, which resulted in subtle changes in the way each shift did things. Several of the miners had independently come up with clever innovations, and naturally some methods were more effective than others.

Leroy was fascinated by how the simple act of breaking down the process into steps and then observing variations allowed him to see the operation from an entirely new perspective. He told me he hadn't enjoyed coming to work so much in years.

It was very enlightening to see how a person with so much knowledge and experience could still significantly shift their mindset.

By the end of the engagement, Leroy, much to his (and my) amazement, had discovered three important insights:

- Their basic mining processes could be substantially improved.

- He needed different information to do his job properly.

- He had to change how he and his managers interacted with their crews.

IT'S TOUGH TO CHANGE HABITS

Anyone who has made New Year's resolutions or embarked on a program to get back in shape understands the difficulty in not just changing but also maintaining a new way of doing things.

There's been a myriad of exercise programs and popular diets over the years, such as Atkins, South Beach, ketogenic, Paleo, and many others. But research shows that 80 percent of dieters will not maintain

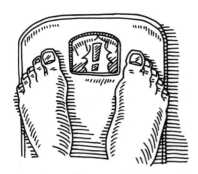

that weight loss for twelve months and will regain more than half of what they lose within two years.[1]

In the business world, there has also been a myriad of improvement methodologies over the years: total quality management, reengineering,

---

1   Daniel Engber, "Unexpected Clues Emerge about Why Diets Fail," *Scientific American*, January 13, 2020, http://www.scientificamerican.com/article/unexpected-clues-emerge-about-why-diets-fail.

theory of constraints, kaizen, Six Sigma, lean, big data, and digital transformation, to name a few.

And similarly, research suggests that roughly 70 percent of all large-scale performance improvement efforts fail.[2] Despite the enormous amount of money invested to improve operating performance, it's still very common to hear the following complaints:

- Digital information technologies fail to improve the quality of information.

- Process reengineering fails to improve overall productivity.

- Sales force management initiatives fail to move the needle on revenue.

- Management training programs fail to change management behavior.

Most senior leaders are painfully aware of these statistics and outcomes, and many have experienced this familiar cycle: A business embarks on a performance improvement project, claims short-term successes, but fails to sustain higher levels of performance. The gains gradually erode until a new technology, a new initiative, or new management arrives.

Then the cycle repeats.

The analogy of individuals trying to get themselves into better shape is like organizations trying to operate at a higher level of performance. An individual wants to lose weight and an organization wants to improve productivity.

The basic math in both cases is output over input. The individual wants to burn more calories and maintain or consume fewer. The

---

2   Michael Bucy, Adrian Finlayson, Greg Kelly, and Chris Moye, "The 'How' of Transformation," McKinsey & Co., May 9, 2016, http://www.mckinsey.com/industries/retail/our-insights/the-how-of-transformation.

business wants to create and sell more products or services at the same or less cost.

For the individual, undergoing such a transformation requires a shift in basic mindsets. It means changing the way you think about eating and exercise. It requires developing a personal program to modify eating and drinking habits and adding more physical activity. It might require a new daily or weekly schedule, which could include behavior changes like waking up earlier to get in a workout, taking the stairs rather than an elevator, or fasting after 7:00 p.m.

Even with this simple example, you can appreciate that trying to improve yourself requires a lifestyle change, not a short-term effort.

In the same way, large-scale improvement initiatives within an organization require a new approach to management. Managers must adopt a different mindset toward their work at every level. And senior leaders must create an environment that fosters this new way of thinking to support their managers' efforts.

THE KEY TO SUSTAINABLE RESULTS

The key to achieving sustainable results is the dynamic management of process, performance, and people. Addressing all three components simultaneously is critical. Each one has an interdependent relationship with the other. Focusing on just one or two components will not yield desired outcomes. It's only by managing all three in a coordinated manner that an organization can achieve long-lasting and meaningful progress.

Our company's president, Dan Lee, likes to use the analogy of a car. "The body of the car represents the organization and its processes. The steering wheel, dashboard, and pedals are the performance system. The driver is the people component. You can't maneuver a vehicle without all three elements working together. If you make significant modifications to any one of them, you need to adjust the other two. If you modify the engine, you need to change other things like tires, electronics, and brakes. You may also need to train the driver how to operate the car at higher speeds."

Business improvement programs routinely fail because they focus only on one or two of these elements. They might improve a process somewhere, but they don't adjust planning parameters. They might install new information software, but the underlying process still dictates the output. Or they might train managers, but without changing the tools or the environment, new skills are difficult to apply.

For roughly thirty years, our consulting company, Carpedia International, has had an unusually high success rate for achieving measurable results in large-scale improvement projects. We've completed over one thousand engagements and worked in a variety of industries (e.g., manufacturing, hotels, retail, insurance, healthcare, technology) on five different continents. More than 90 percent of our engagements have resulted in higher levels of financial and operating performance.

We're often brought in after companies have attempted internal initiatives or invested in new technologies. This has given us a unique perspective to see what works and what doesn't.

We've also worked with brilliant leaders from some of the most successful and well-managed companies in the world. Their insights and ideas have helped shape how we think and how our company provides its services.

The leaders in these companies view process, performance, and people as interrelated elements that must be managed concurrently. They understand that challenges are found in all three areas and that they can't be fixed independently. This balanced and coordinated mindset is a distinguishing characteristic that helps them prosper and flourish, year in and year out, in good times and in bad.

They don't think of improvement as a *destination*. They see it as a journey. They see it as a new way of doing things, which requires new ways to manage. Their overall objective is to achieve better results by continually elevating the management capability of the organization.

EVEN GREAT COMPANIES HAVE CHALLENGES

All organizations are constantly changing in subtle and not-so-subtle ways. Automation, digital technology, and globalization have dramatic impacts on how processes work. Data analysis and artificial intelligence have dramatic impacts on how performance is measured. And technology, diversity, equity, and inclusion all have dramatic impacts on how people are organized and managed.

The advantage of being a consultant is that you get to experience working in many different operating environments and industry sectors, in a wide variety of cultures, and with people with various levels of education.

In time you see, despite all the differences, similar patterns and similar challenges. Some of the insights I first learned working with Leroy have bubbled to the surface time and time again.

All organizations are a collection of processes. Over time, due to complexity, processes operate at only about 60 percent of their capacity. This gap is largely hidden because of the way we build planning factors into our performance systems. 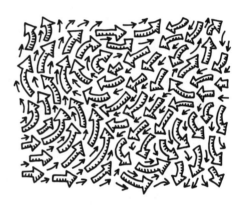 Because of this, managers often believe their resource utilization is significantly better than it is, which doesn't provide the information they need to improve.

Despite technical proficiency, performance systems are not well aligned from strategy to execution. Financial and operating performance indicators are often disconnected. Work that is planned or scheduled on any given day can have little to do with operating budgets for an area. Results are eventually reconciled but often far too late to be useful for managers.

So, although managers are responsible for optimizing processes and performance, the odds are significantly stacked against them. To further complicate things, they're often in their role due to technical experience, not management skills. Without the right tools, training, or information, it's very difficult to continuously improve their areas.

In an era of unprecedented change, competition and technological innovation will continue to force managers to modify the underlying processes that make up their organizations. And as those processes change, the performance systems and management skills must change along with them.

The ability to prosper in this uncertain environment will require a resilient mindset at all levels of the organization.

HOW THIS BOOK IS ORGANIZED

This book was written for senior leaders who need to execute their strategies. The intent is to provide a different way to frame and *think*  about getting results and specifically how the integration of process, performance, and people is critical to develop and implement changes that stick.

At the front of each chapter is a road map that summarizes the point of the chapter, the mindset principle that will get you there, and an overview of the chapter contents. These summaries are usually put at the end of a chapter in business books, but we've placed them up front largely based on a story a client once told me about consultants. I was never sure if it really happened or if it was just some kind of urban legend. Or if he was just giving me a warning.

He told me that one day a consultant was making a presentation to a group of managers, including the president of the organization. After listening for a while, the president began to feel bored and restless. She asked the consultant to get to the point and to tell her the net impact of the recommendations.

Not wanting to be thrown off his agenda, the consultant replied, "Great question, but you're one step ahead of me. I'll cover that a little later in the presentation."

So the president collected her laptop, got up, and walked to the door. As she was leaving, she turned briefly to a colleague and said, "Someone let me know when he gets to that section."

Many of our clients are results-based people. They like the answer up front so that they can draw their own conclusions from the evidence we present. So that's how the book is structured.

It also provides you with the ability to selectively explore what you're interested in.

The book is structured in a sequence that reflects an improvement cycle. It's divided into three parts: Where to Look, What to Improve, and How to Get Results. We'll explore each of these areas and highlight how traditional management thinking leads to disappointing results and then contrast that with the benefits of thinking holistically about process, performance, and people.

WHERE TO LOOK

The Results Equation

Assess the Opportunity

Create a Results Strategy

WHAT TO IMPROVE

Improve Processes

Align Performance

Develop People

HOW TO GET RESULTS

Focus the Effort

Prepare for Change

Implement Change

The Where to Look section discusses the most common challenges we typically find and suggests methods to target improvement. It provides insight into the following questions:

- How do you identify gaps in financial and operating performance?

- How do you quantify the extent of the problems?

- How do you build a project strategy to close the gaps?

The What to Improve section is about the practical steps you need to take to improve various aspects of the organization and build a playbook. It provides insight into the following questions:

- How do you improve operating processes?

- How do you align performance systems?

- How do you coach and train managers to interact with their employees?

The How to Get Results section focuses on how to install changes so that they stick. Some of the questions it addresses include the following:

- How do you align the organization around your plan?

- How do you train your managers to think and act differently?

- How do you implement changes and protect your gains?

Although each section is designed to reinforce and build on the previous one, they can be read independently.

Let's get started.

PART 1

WHERE TO LOOK

WHERE TO LOOK

THE RESULTS EQUATION

Assess the Opportunity

Create a Results Strategy

 WHAT TO IMPROVE

Improve Processes

Align Performance

Develop People

 HOW TO GET RESULTS

Focus the Effort

Prepare for Change

Implement Change

Mindset Principle: Create an Environment for Success

The key to achieving sustainable results is creating an environment that supports the ongoing, dynamic management of process, performance, and people.

RESULTS

process + performance + people

Defining Process

All organizations are made up of processes. A process is simply two or more value-added steps that require a handoff of material or information to create a finished product or service. To maximize productive time, minimize unproductive time.

Defining Performance

Performance refers to the performance system that provides management with information. The objective is to align financial and operating indicators and all levels of management.

Defining People

People refers primarily to management behaviors and employee skills. The objective is to improve the effectiveness of the time that managers spend planning, communicating, following up, and problem-solving, or what we call dynamic management.

THE RESULTS EQUATION

*Excellent firms don't believe in excellence—only in
constant improvement and constant change.*

—TOM PETERS

We were working at an automotive parts manufacturer. One of our consultants observed that the plant had created its own time zone. All the clocks in the plant were set ten minutes ahead of the actual time.

No one knew why or when the practice had started. A long-term employee eventually recalled that the clocks were changed many years before so that shift workers could finish ten minutes early to catch a bus that came on the hour.

After some investigation, it turned out that three years earlier, the bus route had changed but the practice hadn't. This caused a problem at the injection molding machines because in the ten-minute gap, the plastic congealed. That meant the next shift started by having to spend the first fifteen minutes purging the machines.

Management was under pressure to improve plant performance. After being advised of the molding machine problem, they decided to end the early departure practice and implement a "hot change" at the end of the shift so that the machines could keep running.

Three months later, nothing had changed.

Not even the clocks.

It's hard to get people to change behaviors, even when it seems relatively simple. At the auto parts manufacturer, except for senior management, no one wanted to change this operating process. What seemed like a simple change had a multitude of implications throughout the plant and directly impacted the activities of employees, production schedulers, and frontline managers.

Changing the process affected the way crews were scheduled and appeared to ask people to work more than they had previously. The planning standards and staging areas needed to be modified to reflect new output expectations, and managers now had to be physically on the floor at shift change to make sure the transition ran smoothly. Coordinating this among different shifts and different departments was much more complicated than it looked on paper.

We see this scenario play out repeatedly. Few process changes are ever simple. They all have implications on other parts of the organization, and sometimes those implications are far deeper than you realize until you start making changes.

The people who have to orchestrate these complexities day in and day out are the organization's managers.

There's been a lot of thought leadership geared toward managers stretching goals, staying focused, hiring the right people, and motivating their employees. While all these seem like smart things to do, they don't address the practical realities that managers face. Most managers don't have the necessary tools or the training. They don't have the environment they need to support continuous improvement.

Are managers really this important?

An article published several years ago in the *Harvard Business Review* posed the question, "Why do we undervalue competent management?" The study looked at core management practices across thirty-four countries, interviewing more than twelve thousand managers. It had two main findings.

The first was that "achieving operational excellence is still a massive challenge for many organizations," and the second was that gaps in basic management practices resulted in large differences in company performance.

"Better-managed firms are more profitable, grow faster, and are less likely to die. Indeed, moving a firm from the worst 10% to the best 10% of management practices is associated with a $15 million increase in profits, 25% faster annual growth, and 75% higher productivity."[3]

The Gallup Organization had similar findings but framed them in the context of employee engagement. In their article, "Why Great Managers Are so Rare," they discuss two large-scale studies conducted in 2012, which found that only 30 percent of US employees are engaged at work, "and a staggeringly low 13% worldwide are engaged."

---

3   Raffaella Sadun, Nicholas Bloom, and John Van Reenen, "Why Do We Undervalue Competent Management?," *Harvard Business Review*, September–October 2017, https://hbr.org/2017/09/why-do-we-undervalue-competent-management.

One of their main points is that "managers account for at least 70% of variance in employee engagement scores across business units."[4]

Without the right environment, organizations rely too much on the sheer talent of their people. That can work for periods of time, but it won't create a sustainable, high-performance culture.

The key to achieving and maintaining superior results is the ongoing, dynamic management of three key elements: process, performance, and people.

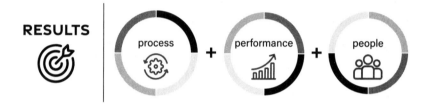

DEFINING RESULTS

Results are the sustained elevation in performance of a targeted indicator. Results can be achieved in any key financial or operating indicator, such as revenue, cost, quality, safety, or service.

Executives often have a clear idea of where they want their organization to be in terms of performance and profitability. The problem is getting to that higher level in a reasonable time.

To drive performance, they turn to their managers and raise performance expectations. If that doesn't work, they spend money on consulting reports or technology solutions, or they build internal improvement teams. We see this pattern because we're often called in

4   Randall J. Beck and Jim Harter, "Why Great Managers Are so Rare," Gallup, accessed March 13, 2023, https://www.gallup.com/workplace/231593/why-great-managers-rare.aspx.

when these efforts stall or when they fail to create sustainable change in performance.

The problem for managers is that they often don't have the time or resources to overcome obstacles. Communicating ideas throughout an organization, getting people to work across functions, physically changing processes and systems, and modifying skills and behaviors of people are time-consuming and difficult. Results are the outcome of coordinated actions.

Consulting companies can suggest useful advice, but they often fail to provide the on-site resources and support that managers need. Reports identify opportunity and spell out what needs to be done, but managers are usually left to do the heavy lifting.

Technology solutions are often limited by the quality of the data that drives them and the way companies selectively use them. Internal improvement teams are often handcuffed by their ability to influence operating managers.

Results, Not Reports, the title of this book, was chosen because it reflects objectives and *how you think about change.* Results are a mindset, and getting and maintaining better results requires humility, courage, passion, and commitment. Improved results don't occur unless something changes, and people don't easily change.

> **Results are a mindset, and getting and maintaining better results requires humility, courage, passion, and commitment.**

It takes humility to see that you can change, it takes courage to do it, it takes passion to lead others, and it takes commitment to stick with it. Results don't just materialize through good intentions. They require an intentional and deliberate change in how you manage.

DEFINING PROCESS

All organizations are made up of processes. A process is simply a series of steps that produce something. In business it usually means a handoff of material or information to create a finished product or service. Each process step contains activities that convert what an organization does into value for their customers, using resources such as material, equipment, labor, and space.

Defining processes is quite complicated. Most organizations are set up in vertical functions, like sales or production, but most processes flow horizontally and touch several different functions. Where a process starts, and where it ends, is a matter of opinion.

It helps to understand the basic type of organization. At the highest level, there are a few product-based organizations commonly  referred to as job shops, batch, and continuous flow. Service-based organizations share similarities but are referred to differently. They have names like professional services, service factories, or continual service operations.

Job shops and professional service organizations are make-to-order operations that create special (or nonstandard) products or services. Product-based examples include custom furniture or commercial printers. Service-based examples might be law, engineering, or consulting. The focus for these types of environments is the utilization of key personnel or resources.

Batch-oriented businesses or service factories are make-to-stock operations that produce similar products or services in large batches. Product-based businesses could be automotive or computer factories.

Service factories might be hospitals, insurance, or banking. The focus for these types of processes is generally to balance their volumes, often centering on scheduling and inventory processes.

Continuous flow-type operations produce standardized products or services in large scale with little or no interruption. Examples of these types of operations would be oil, gas, or milk processing. In the service world, examples might be retail, automated warehousing, and digital services. The focus here is usually on uptime, speed, and throughput.

MINDSET PRINCIPLE: INCREASE WRENCH TIME

One of the key concepts for processes and how to improve them is the concept of wrench time.

Early in my career, I was working in a maintenance department, and I asked a veteran project director what I should be looking for to improve the process. He said, "The same thing you look for in every area: wrench time."

He went on to explain that the business world is full of people with titles. Their titles represent special skills they've learned, but they don't use those skills enough: salespeople don't spend enough time selling; managers don't spend enough time managing; and mechanics don't spend enough time with a wrench in their hands—or what he referred to as wrench time.

He continued, "The secret to performance improvement in any area is to try to increase wrench time. Identify the obstacles that prevent a person from using their core skill more frequently.

"A mechanic loses time waiting for assignments, not having the right supplies on hand, or traveling around the property. Different assignment methods, tool preparation, or layout changes free up valuable wrench time. A salesperson may simply not have enough leads. Or they may spend too much time on administration or traveling to meetings. Managers aren't given the tools they need to do their job effectively.

"In every case, if you can figure out how to free up or capture time and convert it into wrench time, performance should improve."

The wrench time logic applies equally well to equipment and other resources.

We were working for a hospital to help increase throughput of their mammography unit. There was a significant wait time for appointments, which was causing them to lose patients to other hospitals.

The key constraint was the limited number of diagnostic machines, which were being utilized at over 95 percent of their available time, at least based on the reported numbers. Studying the process in detail identified that a significant portion of the time was actually being taken up by physicians counseling patients in the same room as the equipment.

The actual equipment usage, or wrench time, was about 40 percent of its capacity. The solution to increase throughput was to have physicians counsel patients in a separate room, freeing up the mammography machines.

Of course, it wasn't that simple, as changes never are. It meant modifying space in the department and scheduling physicians differently.

In chapter 4, we'll examine several ways to capture wrench time in an organization.

DEFINING PERFORMANCE

Performance refers to the performance management system. Like processes, there are different types of performance management systems that are tailored to support the operating environment.

Job shops or professional service organizations have project management or work order-based systems. Batch-type operations have more classical production scheduling systems, and continuous flow-type operations have systems geared to managing uptime.

One way to think about performance management systems is in terms of a time continuum. Everything moves either forward or backward from the point of execution. The point of execution is that point in time when value is added to a product or when a service is delivered to a customer.

All organizations try to ensure that the point of execution is effective and predictable. The more predictable the point of execution, the easier it is to optimize resources and to deliver a consistent experience to customers. The less predictable, the more resources are required and the more variable the customer experience.

This predictability is highly dependent on how well the various performance systems align. As the following diagram illustrates, each level of the organization manages different aspects of the performance system.

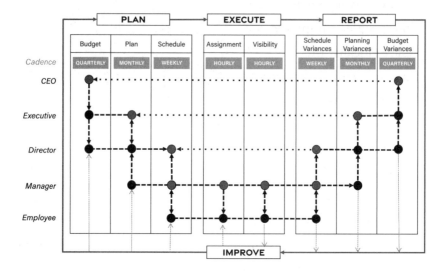

Senior leaders tend to deal with longer-range planning of resources that are built around how revenue and costs flow through the business. Middle-level managers take these financial guidelines and build out midterm resource plans. The front line manages the activities needed to deliver a product or service.

Unfortunately, operating activities are prone to variability, and when that happens, alignment starts to break down.

MINDSET PRINCIPLE: SYNCHRONIZE LEADERSHIP

The key concept for performance is synchronizing leadership. Properly integrated performance systems are arguably the most important tool that the chief executive officer (CEO) has for aligning an organization.

Performance systems are an integrated control tool that translates the strategic plans of a company into specific activities and account-abilities required within the organization.

They link operating activities to financial systems and allow management to minimize unplanned variances in the process. They also optimize company resources like people, equipment, or space. Ideally, they help all management levels plan, execute, report, and improve their area of responsibility in accordance with the CEO's strategic direction.

But alignment is elusive for many organizations.

For reasons we'll cover in chapter 5, performance systems get disconnected between financial planning and operational execution. Daily work plans and schedules that managers use to control their areas are created from operating parameters that often have little resemblance to the financial objectives of the organization.

This is a result of how planning systems are built and maintained and how frontline managers need to react to the realities of their operating world.

Without proper alignment, it's very difficult for a manager to effectively plan work. Without decent planning tools, it's impossible for managers to provide the right assignments to their employees, to follow up, to coach, and to do all the things senior leaders need them to do to get results and to continuously improve.

In chapter 5, we'll look at how performance management systems get unaligned and some of the things you can do to straighten them out.

DEFINING PEOPLE

People refers primarily to management behaviors and employee skills.

Managers are responsible for ensuring that processes run as well as they can, using the least resources possible while delivering consistent and predictable results. Managers are dependent on performance systems to provide information to help them plan, execute, and measure results. They, in turn, use this information to manage the process and to coach and train their staff.

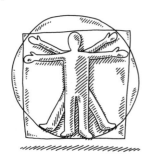

Peter Drucker once wrote, "The productivity of work is not the responsibility of the worker but of the manager." Over the years, we've learned to appreciate and understand what he meant.

Drucker's point was illustrated by Jan Carlzon, CEO of SAS Airlines from 1981 to 1994, who came up with the idea that a company's organizational chart should be inverted. Carlzon believed that managers should be at the bottom and frontline employees at the top with appropriate decision-making ability.

The basic concept was to recognize that managers work for employees—and not the other way around. The framework was adopted to varying degrees by several large organizations.

The diagram itself never really caught on. Upside-down organizational charts did look awkward, but it's too bad because the idea was a good one. Visually, they made an important point that is often lost. The key to being a good manager is to remove obstacles that keep your employees from being more effective. After all, they're the people who sell, service, design, fabricate, store, ship, and deliver products and services that generate revenue.

Many business books talk about good and bad leaders, but they tend to focus on people's attributes or characteristics (persuasive, humble, charismatic, bold, visionary, etc.).

These are no doubt important and influence how a manager behaves. But behaviors themselves are more basic and specific than that. It's the things managers

> The key to being a good manager is to remove obstacles that keep your employees from being more effective.

physically do. How they plan, assign, follow up, actively listen, train, coach, problem solve, or track performance.

We spend a lot of time watching people work in a plant or an office to better understand how work moves through an organization. From this vantage point, you see many problems that crop up throughout the day and how workers and managers interact to try to fix them.

You often can't help but notice that managers are often in their position due to technical skills, not management skills. Which, if you think about it, is a little like a sports team promoting its leading scorer to coach.

As a result, companies lose their best practitioners and end up with people in management positions who are more comfortable physically doing the tasks than they are at managing others.

You also run into something called the Peter Principle, named after Dr. Laurence J. Peter. The Peter Principle was a satiric observation that you keep getting promoted in an organization until you reach your level of incompetence (the skills you've acquired along the way are eventually inadequate for your role).

Like all good satire, there is some truth to this. Most of the management training expense in organizations goes to frontline managers, but each level of management in an organization can suffer from the same process and information shortcomings we've discussed.

MINDSET PRINCIPLE: DEVELOP DYNAMIC MANAGEMENT

We call the engagement time between a manager and an employee dynamic management. According to *Oxford*, dynamic means "continuously changing and progressing." A dynamic person is someone

who has a "positive attitude and is full of energy and new ideas."

To understand what dynamic management is, it's helpful to think of the role of a Hollywood film director. When a studio is filming, the director may not be doing any of the acting, but they still play a significant role in the outcome of the movie.

There are many important people involved, including writers, actors, and camera and lighting crew, all with very different skill sets. The director "directs" the various people and activities involved. They coordinate, provide expectations, coach, correct, and influence the environment to achieve a finished product. The director manages the dynamics of the environment.

DYNAMIC MANAGEMENT

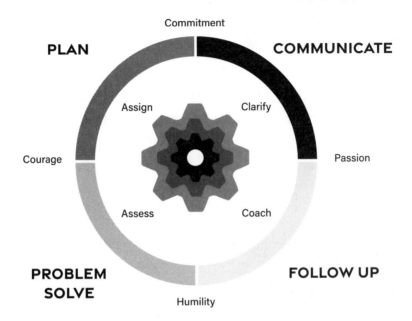

The term *dynamic management* refers to the continuous and evolving interaction between a manager and an employee. It involves assigning work, following up on progress, providing coaching, and correcting mistakes.

Dynamic management is the seemingly obvious part of managing people. Yet this activity simply doesn't happen very much.

In one study we spent over eighteen hundred hours observing managers in a wide variety of industries. We found that less than 10 percent of their time consisted of dynamic management. The rest of their day is taken up by touring, firefighting, administration, or doing direct work that could be done by others.

This is not due to a lack of desire but rather a lack of tools and infrastructure to manage differently.

The key to dynamic management is to focus on the specific interaction between managers and their staff, which requires decent planning and a clear understanding of the role of management as supporting staff, not monitoring them.

Chapter 6 discusses common challenges faced by managers and employees and explores how organizations can improve the environment to promote dynamic management.

WHERE TO LOOK

The Results Equation

ASSESS THE OPPORTUNITY

Create a Results Strategy

 # WHAT TO IMPROVE

Improve Processes

Align Performance

Develop People

 # HOW TO GET RESULTS

Focus the Effort

Prepare for Change

Implement Change

CHAPTER 2: ASSESS THE OPPORTUNITY

Mindset Principle: Find the Gaps

The assessment links critical key financial and operating indicators to identify gaps in current performance and to identify recoverable opportunity. It provides a business case and an overall strategy to improve the organization's results.

Link Finance and Operations

- Revenue

- Cost

- Capital

Evaluate Operating Performance

- Determine productive and nonproductive time

- Study the alignment of the performance system

- Observe how managers interact with their staff

Build a Business Case

- Assess potential improvement

- Develop an overall strategy

- Create a work plan

- Develop a cash flow plan

ASSESS THE OPPORTUNITY

Even if you are on the right track, you'll get run over if you just sit there.
—WILL ROGERS

had a sales meeting with an executive for a company headquartered in London, England. We met in the lobby, and he ushered me into his office. He asked me to grab a seat while he got some coffee for the two of us.

TRAFALGAR SQUARE.

He had a beautiful office with a stunning view of Trafalgar Square. The office had modern furnishings, which were a stark contrast to the mahogany paneling in the lobby and the historic building itself. The desk was a simple glass table with a chair on either side.

It was one of the few sunny days on my trip, and brilliant light streamed through the window. I sat down and took the opportunity to absorb the magnificent view of the busy square. The executive returned with the coffee.

As a casual conversation starter, I said, "I've been in many interesting offices, but this may be the best view I've ever seen."

The executive placed the coffee down on the table and replied, "Thanks. Now get out of my chair."

Like the part in a movie where the plot twist is revealed, all the missed clues suddenly became painfully apparent (particularly the placement of a notepad and family photograph). I had made the simple assumption that the executive would have his back to the window. Precisely because of the view, this executive had chosen to face the window.

A fairly heavy awkwardness followed as I collected my things and moved to the other side of the desk.

It's hard not to make assumptions.

There are all sorts of common biases we all suffer from. Confirmation, framing, anchoring, pattern recognition, and self-interest are some of the more common ones. They all tend to lead us to embrace evidence that supports our thinking and to reject evidence that doesn't.

As you become more familiar with any subject matter, you're more likely to cut corners or to jump to conclusions without considering all the facts.

When we're brought in by organizations to assess where they could improve, senior executives almost always have a good sense of what they want to achieve. They bring us in, in part, to get away from their own biases. What they want from us is a fresh perspective to identify *where* that improvement should come from and what's required to get it.

We have our own biases, of course, but being an outside entity helps because it means we're forced to gather facts to form our opinions, and we aren't weighed down by politics or organizational memory.

To provide executives with this perspective, we perform an opportunity assessment. It's a kind of operational due diligence to determine whether there are opportunities where we can help, above and beyond what they're already doing.

The basic concept is to assess the performance of the operating environment and to link historical outcomes to the organization's financial results. The assessment provides a snapshot of the operational health of an organization and an analysis of where they could improve.

The purpose of the assessment is to quantify the magnitude of opportunity and to determine what portion of it could be recovered. The purpose is *not* to identify solutions. Solutions are developed later with the input of operating managers and employees.

The assessment provides a project approach and identifies the base period so that performance changes can be measured.

LINK FINANCE AND OPERATIONS

To understand the financial numbers and to determine what operating activities drive them, you need to create a profit driver model.

At the highest level, focus on three financial areas that determine profitability of the organization: revenue, cost, and capital efficiency.

But the financial numbers on their own aren't overly helpful, so you need to dig deeper into the underlying drivers of those outcomes and connect the financial and operating worlds together.

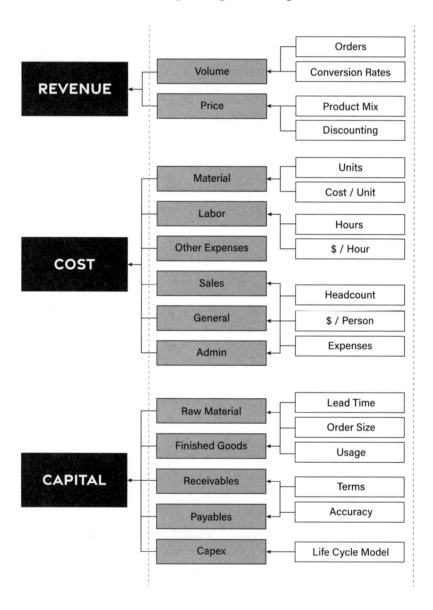

Linking Financial and Operational Indicators

IDENTIFY THE TRENDS AND GAPS

The diagram illustrates the connection between financial and operating indicators for a typical manufacturing business.

For all relevant financial indicators, study two to three years of historical data to identify trends and anomalies and to examine how well they correlate to the corresponding operating indicators. If they're available, financial performance can be benchmarked against competitive sets, but if not, simply benchmark the company against itself.

Study good and bad performance periods and try to understand what happened.

REVENUE

Review the organization's overall sales numbers by customer segments and sales channels. If possible, break down these aggregate numbers into the number of units sold and the average price per order. Analyze the links between what the sales and the service people are doing and how those activities impact revenue.

From an operating perspective, opportunities are identified by analyzing what's commonly referred to as sales funnels.

SALES FUNNEL

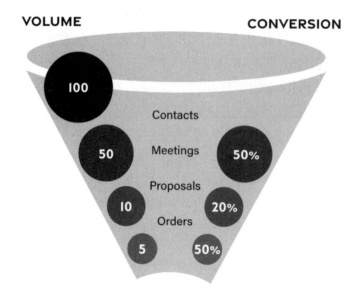

All customer segments and sales channels can be analyzed by these funnels, which simply reflect how individual companies in the total served market eventually make their way down through the funnel to become customers. The key drivers for each stage in the funnel are the volume of potential customers entering that stage and the ability of the organization to convert them to the next stage.

Marketing efforts are directed mostly at the top of the funnel, and sales and service efforts are generally more toward the middle and bottom of the funnel. The difficulty is that there isn't always clean and accurate information for each stage of the funnel. Companies try to maintain this through their customer relationship management systems, but it takes a lot of discipline to keep this information accurate and up to date.

Nonetheless, the assessment must make connections between revenue performance and the various stages of the funnel. How well a company generates leads is reflected by the number of prospects and by the types of prospects that enter the sales funnel.

How well the company sells is reflected by the conversion at each stage of the funnel. If either volumes or conversion rates can be improved, then revenue should improve.

On the pricing side, the first step is to figure out how pricing decisions are made. The pricing process is often not well defined in many organizations. Pricing is a powerful way to improve profit without the need for large-scale culture change.

It's often quoted that a 1 percent improvement in price is worth a 10 percent improvement in productivity. Given that there is so much effort involved in trying to raise productivity by 10 percent, it's somewhat surprising that price isn't the first thing performance improvement groups focus on. But like the problem that many start-ups experience when they use similar math—"All we need to be profitable is a one percent market share"—getting that 1 percent gain is very difficult.

There are a few different ways that organizations determine pricing. Some apply a cost-plus logic, but accurate cost allocations make this practice difficult. Other companies set prices based on what they believe customers are willing to pay or on what their competitors are charging.

Actual negotiated pricing is highly variable and significantly influenced by the relative importance of the customer, what competitors do in bid situations, what procurement departments demand, the size and scale of the sale, future opportunities, etc. Prices are also influenced by personal relationships and even by sales compensation plans. All these factors result in a range in which prices for a certain product or service vary.

From an assessment point of view, understand whether high variation exists. Much like waste in a process, the opportunity in pricing often lies in the variation.

Variation is driven by people's behaviors, which are influenced by incentives. Pricing control is often distributed throughout an organization, and various people at different levels are allowed to discount from a benchmark. Identifying where prices are discounted and trying to understand what drives that behavior are insightful.

Raising prices is notoriously hard in many industries, but the objective is to increase the average price, not to raise prices. So if you can reduce discounting, you can reduce the variation and improve the average price.

COST

From the trend analysis, you should get a sense of what is happening to costs relative to revenues. This identifies potential areas for more detailed review. The basic cost areas examined in an assessment are material, labor, and overheads.

These areas lend themselves to financial and operating analysis. Material studies focus on procurement practices, yield, and waste. Labor studies quantify productivity or look at skills variation. Overhead studies review overall direct versus indirect positions, management spans of control, and various costs as they relate to revenues.

Variable overhead costs include things like electricity usage. Often these costs are driven by the number of hours an organization operates. If an improvement project reduces the number of hours needed to operate, it will also reduce some of these costs.

A few finance directors have pointed out to us that one quick way to reduce some variable costs would be to stop hiring people like us. As you can imagine, it's not our intention to put a spotlight on fee-based services, but recurring professional fees do have a way of drifting upward over time.

The studies conducted can be tailored to cost areas that are increasing over time or that are assumed to be high based on competitive benchmarks.

CAPITAL

Assessing capital efficiency takes numerous forms. We generally focus on working capital to determine how well cash is being optimized. Look at what is happening over time to the cash cycle and operationally review receivables and payables functions.

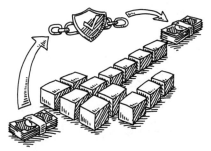

Managing cash is exceptionally important when organizations are growing because of the financial demands that growth creates. Its importance is sometimes even more pronounced in a downturn if you don't have much of it.

Inventory management goes up on the priority list when interest rates and corresponding carrying costs are high. Even when interest rates are low, for many organizations, inventory is a significant asset on the balance sheet.

To uncover opportunity in this area, one approach is to quantify the ideal inventory level. There are several analytical techniques to try to marry up current levels against forecast requirements. Once a reasonable level has been established, you can determine how much is excess.

The cause of excess inventory is usually split between planning parameters and people's behaviors. The planning parameters (e.g., forecasting, lead times, service levels, safety stock levels, accuracy, and order quantities) require technical analysis, and all can yield opportunities.

Organizations tend to add fixed costs as they grow. For fixed overhead costs, a basic approach for finding opportunity is to challenge the notion that fixed costs really are fixed. Variable costs are often targeted in improvement projects because it's easier to see how they fluctuate with respect to volume.

While fixed costs are not linear, there is a step-change relationship to growth. One analytical technique is to look back to a time when the organization was more profitable at similar revenue volumes. Understanding how overhead costs changed over time and the underlying reasons why can lead to opportunities to remove overhead costs that have not added value.

We're sometimes asked to help answer questions about where and how the organization should deploy its capital, such as network configurations in their supply chains. But these types of studies are more strategic in nature and usually come from a specific request rather than from a general improvement assessment.

EVALUATE OPERATING PERFORMANCE
DETERMINE PRODUCTIVE AND NONPRODUCTIVE TIME

We spend a lot of time observing workflows to identify operating challenges and to quantify productivity levels. At any given time, a process is either up or down. It's either productive and creating value of some kind or it's not. It's like the wrench time analogy. Ideally you want to maximize the uptime.

Productive time, also sometimes referred to as value-added, is time spent that the customer would be willing to pay for. Nonproductive time is the time people spend reworking, firefighting, expediting, or doing something because there's a breakdown somewhere else in the process. It might have to be done, and it can be hard work; it just doesn't add much value.

Productive time typically takes up about 60 to 70 percent of the process and nonproductive about 30 to 40 percent. It surprises most managers to learn how much time falls into this second bucket. This is because people often equate productive time with effort, but the two aren't necessarily related. Nonproductive time can take as much or more effort than productive time.

No process is ever 100 percent productive. A portion of nonproductive time is necessary to allow some flexibility of operations. Even highly automated and so-called world-class processes have 10 to 15 percent of nonproductive time due to real-life variability and planned downtime.

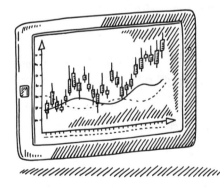

Observations are augmented with data analysis. Many technologies have been developed that capture process flow analytics, such as barcode scanners, magnetic stripe readers, proximity, and smart card readers. These data sources provide capture points to support historical volume analysis, to compare what is being observed with similar periods, and to help identify capacities throughout a process.

The assessment quantifies the nonproductive time and targets some portion for recovery. The portion of time that can be recovered is based on historical experience in that type of process and industry but is usually up to one-third of the total nonproductive time observed.

Part of the operating assessment might include indirect support functions. These functions keep organizations working, but it's not always easy to determine how many people are needed in each one.

A question to ask is whether the organization has any tools to determine how many indirect people are required. Often the number of indirect staff is driven by historical rules of thumb or as a reaction to some previous service failure. This leads to areas being staffed to what is essentially their peak workload conditions.

STUDY THE ALIGNMENT OF THE PERFORMANCE SYSTEM

The second key area where we find common challenges is in the performance information that is available for managers. Unfortunately, the lack of alignment between executive planning and frontline planning is one of the most common challenges we come across.

Performance systems are designed to help leaders plan, execute, and report on results. The senior leadership team is responsible for the business and financial plan and for setting the overall objectives for the functional areas below.

Middle managers determine how to acquire and allocate operating resources (equipment or people) to achieve the plan. Frontline leaders build and manage work schedules to reflect the forecast volume of work. Each level of planning has corresponding accountability and reporting.

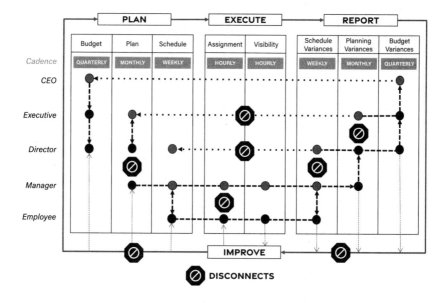

Performance system challenges usually start with a basic disconnect between finance and operations. Key planning tools include budgets, forecasts, work plans, and work schedules. For all of these to be effectively integrated, you need accurate planning standards and reasonable mathematical relationships among revenue dollars, functional volumes, and activities.

Alignment among these elements is frequently poor. Often frontline managers have no clear understanding of how their day-to-day work (or the key performance indicators they measure) impacts the financial results of the company.

The tool most companies use to try to tie the finance and operating worlds together is the operating budget. But key performance indicators that are tracked in the operating world tend to be activity-based, whereas budgets are often dollar-based. This makes it difficult to translate sales or volume forecasts into specific resource requirements.

For example, a budget might forecast a 10 percent growth in sales, but it often doesn't identify what is required to get that 10 percent growth. Grow or retain existing customers? Get more new customers? At a practical level, what does this mean in terms of service activities, marketing efforts, or sales calls? Those tend to be the things managers at the front line measure.

Functional groups often don't trust sales forecasts, and they create their own guidelines based on historical experience. Work planning standards are often inaccurate, or processes have changed, and standards aren't up to date. They're rarely owned by frontline managers, and as a result, they're frequently challenged or overridden.

And as we've discussed, operating issues can get baked into planning numbers if budgets are built off last year's actual performance.

At the other end of the performance system, there often isn't a good improvement feedback loop. Improved processes (from creative ideas from employees or modified equipment) aren't always tied back into future planning parameters.

The fact that many existing operating challenges are effectively hidden makes it difficult for managers to identify or fix them. It also short-circuits the way they think about process improvement and their ability to improve their areas of responsibility.

Aligning incentives can be another challenge. Sometimes decisions made about the key objectives and measurements for functional areas, or positions, get everyone in the boat rowing in a different direction. Some of the more common ones we see include the following:

- Salespeople are incentivized on volume that doesn't match the capacity of the operation.

- Engineers and architects create designs that complicate future operating requirements.

- Materials managers minimize inventory by increasing the replenishment frequency, but this increases freight and handling costs.

- Procurement consolidates suppliers or parts ordering, but this results in higher inventory levels.

- Production increases stocking locations to reduce downtime, but this increases stock and labor requirements.

- Decisions to eliminate slow or obsolete stock negatively impact finance balance sheets and customer service (holding items in inventory for older products or past customers).

The unfortunate result of these various challenges is that the management levels of an organization become unaligned. With poor alignment, there is little incentive and no systematic way for leaders or managers to drive continuous improvement.

OBSERVE HOW MANAGERS INTERACT WITH THEIR STAFF

Managers control most of the resources that a company consumes. The decisions they routinely make are critical to ensure that things run smoothly and on plan. As a result, how they physically behave day-to-day is important.

To understand this, we conduct management studies. The purpose of the study is to quantify how a manager spends their time and where they spend their time. How effective the performance management system is will generally dictate the type of management behaviors to expect.

These studies tell you a lot about the nature of an organization and its culture.

It shows you how managers and employees interact—and how well the management tools support the manager. These are all useful insights into what existing behaviors help or hinder the effectiveness of the organization.

Spending time walking in their shoes allows you to answer some of these questions:

- How does the manager plan work?

- How is work assigned?

- How is the work controlled to the plan?

- How does the manager communicate to their people or to other departments?

The opportunity is to shift some of their time to more dynamic management. This is done by clarifying their role, refining the performance management system tools required, and training and coaching them to manage their environment differently.

BUILD A BUSINESS CASE

For executives to determine whether it makes sense to pursue any improvement opportunity, the assessment needs to identify the expected value to the organization.

ASSESS POTENTIAL IMPROVEMENT

Based on the observations and detailed analysis of financial and operational indicators, an

For executives to determine whether it makes sense to pursue any improvement opportunity, the assessment needs to identify the expected value to the organization.

improvement range can be determined. The potential improvement is calculated, at a high level, by determining a percentage improvement on targeted indicators and relating this to how revenue or costs will be impacted.

The improvement objective doesn't assume to fix all the challenges that were quantified, but it does identify a portion of the total opportunity assessed. This recovery portion can vary significantly by process, functional area, and industry.

Consultants sometimes have an advantage determining this number if they have experienced comparable situations in similar organizations. As a general guideline, most organizations have the

capacity to improve up to about one-third of the improvement identified in any given area.

The remaining capacity can be targeted later in continuous improvement efforts.

DEVELOP AN OVERALL STRATEGY

The overall strategy helps to define not only the logic of the plan but also the potential consequences.

Different types of organizations require different types of strategies. In job shops or professional service environments, the strategy centers around how to effectively manage the backlog of work to maximize the utilization of key resources.

The basic idea is to make improvements to the planning process to remove downtime, resulting in more output and possibly lower backlogs. Ultimately there will be fewer resources required or a need for more volume.

There are a few adjacent effects that must be considered.

- If you lower the backlogs of work, does it give you any potential advantages that can be exploited?
- Can you improve your service levels?
- Will it change what you sell or change your pricing?
- Can you reduce resources and maintain backlog levels?
- Can you sell more to offset the backlog reduction?
- How does all of this affect your overhead costs?

In a batch or service factory type of environment, where the process is capacity- and activity-driven, the focus is to manage and schedule workloads as efficiently as possible. A batch operation tries to maximize material and inventory efficiency to optimize the flow of work.

The strategy must answer the question of how you will make improvements to the assignment and planning requirements of the organization. The outcome should be a more balanced workload with fewer resources needed.

- Can you capitalize on this with increased volume?
- Are there any capacity constraints?
- Should you reduce processing hours?

In a more fluid continuous flow or mass service environment, the objective is to maximize uptime and throughput. With an uptime strategy, you're targeting improvements in the process or planning to remove downtime, resulting in more volume out and reduced lead times.

Like the others, thought needs to be put into what to do with the increased throughput.

- Can it be sold? Will it increase inventories?

- Will it reduce costs by reducing the processing hours required? Will shorter cycle times increase potential customers?

- Will it strain suppliers' delivery capabilities?

CREATE A WORK PLAN

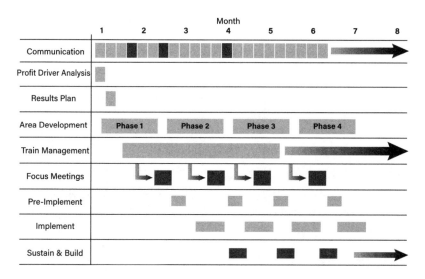

A Typical Improvement Project

Work plans can vary by area and focus, but the basic construct is similar. There is a development phase that builds from the initial assessment with key meetings to make sure everyone is brought along, training and prototyping in advance of major changes, an implementation phase, and a follow-up period.

Communication at various levels needs to happen throughout. The more difficult aspect is determining who will be involved and the time commitment required.

The time required to do the project can be supplied by both internal and external resources. External or internal consultants can help with groundwork and project management, but organizations must commit leadership and operating people to an improvement initiative if they want it to be successful.

Many change initiatives fail due to lukewarm support from important executives or department leaders or due to a lack of commitment to provide enough time or resources to area managers.

DEVELOP A CASH FLOW PLAN

Improvement never happens overnight, so there's always a lag between starting a project and generating measurable results.

> Many change initiatives fail due to lukewarm support from important executives or department leaders or due to a lack of commitment to provide enough time or resources to area managers.

If the organization is using outside resources or making capital investments as part of the initiative, then a cash flow analysis should be developed to understand the costs associated with the project and when results will materialize.

Many organizations misjudge when results will materialize. Key indicators and financial improvement are not always directly correlated. There are many factors that need to be considered, which we'll discuss in the next chapter.

The cost side of the equation is based on the project plan and includes the time that must be committed by those involved. The cost for internal resources depends on whether people are taken out their positions and need to be backfilled. External resources can be based on time and materials or some form of performance-based arrangement.

Any potential capital expenditures can also be assessed, although a working premise of this book is that most organizations can better optimize their existing assets and resources and usually don't require additional capital expenditures.

WHERE TO LOOK

The Results Equation

Assess the Opportunity

CREATE A RESULTS STRATEGY

WHAT TO IMPROVE

Improve Processes

Align Performance

Develop People

HOW TO GET RESULTS

Focus the Effort

Prepare for Change

Implement Change

Mindset Principle: Cash the Check

The Results Strategy articulates, in practical terms, how results will be achieved and how the impact will be seen in key indicators and financial statements. It identifies potential issues and complications, early in the initiative, that need to be considered. The strategy also sets expectations regarding what people should expect in terms of activities, focus, timing, and participation.

Identify the Focus Areas

- Revenue-based initiatives

- Cost-based initiatives

- Capital-based initiatives

Determine How to Measure Results

- Make sure savings are real

- Get the baseline right

- Review the link to incentives

Develop a Communication Strategy

- Stakeholder communication

- Employee engagement

CREATE A RESULTS STRATEGY

Strategy is not the consequence of planning,
but the opposite: its starting point.
—HENRY MINTZBERG

One of our early clients asked us if we were interested in helping him develop a strategy for one of his company's divisions. We said, "Of course." He told us that the division was making money, but on its current trajectory, it wouldn't be where he wanted it to be in three years.

He said they would grow their profits by 25 percent, but he wanted to double that amount.

Without asking enough questions, we drew up a proposal that laid out a fairly classical approach to developing a strategy. The proposal looked at studying the current market situation, identifying strengths and weaknesses, establishing goals and objectives, and then developing specific action plans.

We reviewed it with him. When he finally looked up from the desk, we couldn't tell whether he was impressed or slightly frustrated. We found out soon enough.

He said, "Too textbook, guys. I don't need you to spend time and money analyzing the marketplace. I want you to figure out how to practically get from A to B."

Nodding in agreement, without really understanding what he was saying, we asked him to explain what he meant. He said that most strategies he'd come across in his career were too generic. "Everyone says that they'll improve customer service and employee satisfaction, reduce cost, and grow revenue. But usually not enough thought goes into what that actually means."

He explained how he would approach developing a strategy. We listened intently, furiously making notes while at the same time trying to look slightly disinterested. He drew two lines on a piece of paper. Both started at the same place. The lower one was fairly flat, and the higher one arched upward.

Pointing to the lower line, he said, "This is where we'll be if we just keep doing what we're doing." Then he pointed to the higher line and said, "This is where our shareholders want us to be. The gap between those two needs a strategy. Can we get there on our own? What do we need to do differently? Sell more? Change our pricing? Be more productive? Where? How? Do we change suppliers? Do we need to acquire a company? We may still need to look at the competitive environment, but figure out some of those questions first."

The assessment we discussed in the previous chapter provides the two lines he drew on the paper. The assessment identifies some of the operating challenges and puts a stake in the ground for where the organization wants to get to.

It tells you *what* the results should be, but it doesn't tell you *how* to get there.

On our projects, we have something we call a Results Strategy that is created within the first five weeks of an engagement. The document is a summary of the tactics needed to achieve results that are identified in the assessment. Its purpose is to break down each of the improvement targets and explain how, in practical terms, the organization will realize the benefits.

It communicates what needs to happen in focus areas, what specific actions are required, who is accountable, and what issues the organization might face. It also outlines how results will be measured and the communication strategy for the initiative. For the project team, the Results Strategy is a working road map and a problem-solving tool that guides how to allocate time and resources.

The Results Strategy forces you, early in the initiative, to address many tough questions that need to be asked. There are numerous potential hurdles and complications that can get in the way.

You have to anticipate and think through these issues early because sometimes decisions need to be made well in advance of actions. There are often multiple stakeholders impacted by those decisions. Thinking through the implications early changes how you align and communicate to stakeholders throughout the change process.

Achieving real results is not for the faint of heart.

The questions we ask, although the terminology is starting to become a little outdated, are these: How will the organization cash the check? How can they convert potential improvement into measurable, tangible results? To get measurable results from an improvement project, you have to think through how those results are going to be captured and where you will be able to see their impact on financial statements.

Cashing the check often requires you to make difficult decisions.

> Cashing the check often requires you to make difficult decisions.

IDENTIFY THE FOCUS AREAS

From the profit drivers being targeted, you determine the focus of the initiative and identify specific work areas. This is the link where the financial world and the operating world come together. It's not always a clean link, as many functional areas impact one another.

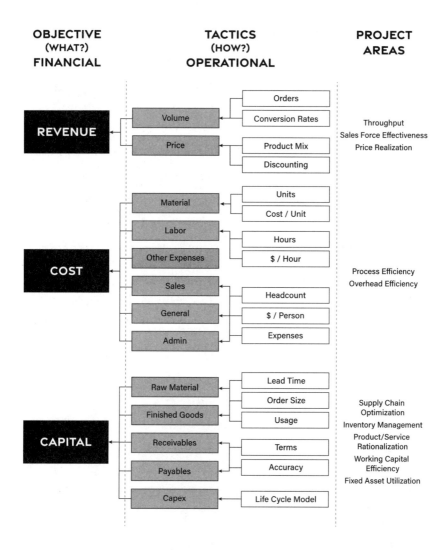

| OBJECTIVE (WHAT?) FINANCIAL | TACTICS (HOW?) OPERATIONAL | | PROJECT AREAS |

If a company is trying to improve its profitability, the general strategy is to either grow revenue or reduce costs. To grow revenue, the more common focus areas would be to increase throughput, improve sales force management, or increase pricing. If the intent is to reduce costs, focus areas are generally designed to improve process or overhead efficiency.

For each focus area, you need to articulate where and how measurable results will be achieved.

REVENUE-BASED INITIATIVES

Many improvement initiatives target cost rather than revenue. Cost reduction is relatively straightforward, at least intellectually, and there are many process measurements available. Revenue improvement is often perceived as having more risk. Sales cycles are usually lengthy, which means that achieving results takes longer than one that focuses on costs.

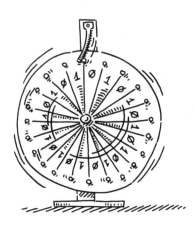

Revenue can be a little nebulous—often more art than science—and measurements are generally strong at the outcome level but weak through the actual revenue process. However, it's precisely this fuzzy aspect of revenue that makes it an area where opportunities exist.

Revenue is a complex topic that involves both strategic decisions (e.g., which products and which markets) and more tactical operational issues (e.g., how we market and sell to targeted customers). To be effective, these projects need to encompass both marketing and selling aspects.

If the assessment identified revenue improvement as an objective, the strategy needs to determine what that actually means. At the highest level, is the plan to sell more or increase prices? If the plan is to sell more, is the increase expected to come from existing accounts or new accounts?

If the plan is to get new customers, the strategy needs to identify how that's going to happen. Often there's an assumption that increasing selling activity will directly lead to growth. But that's not always the case. Does the organization have enough leads? Do they need to modify the way product or market segments are divided or targeted? Which customers are being targeted?

Those questions impact what the marketing group is doing. Sales management projects sometimes shy away from marketing aspects because they're often different functional areas, but that ignores several key drivers of sales activities.

John Wanamaker, a US department store merchant, famously complained, "Half the money I spend on advertising is wasted; the trouble is I don't know which half." He said that about one hundred years ago, but it still resonates with many people today. Despite the difficulty in establishing clear cause and effect, marketing plays a big role in customer targeting.

If the plan is to increase sales volumes with existing customers, the strategy must identify how that will happen. Bigger orders? Is the plan to upsell or cross-sell? Improve service to retain more of the customer base? Take business from competitors? Will it be from new products or services?

Many companies struggle to increase business from existing customers for a couple of reasons. The first is that it usually means taking business directly away from competitors. Unless the company has distinct advantages, taking business away from competitors requires time and often leads to lowering prices, which damages profitability.

The second reason is that customers often intentionally divide their purchases between alternate sources to optimize their own leverage and reduce risk. Companies are generally more successful increasing sales volume with existing accounts when those accounts are themselves growing and they manage to maintain or grow their share of that business. In these cases, smarter customer targeting might be needed.

Sales force management initiatives focus on improving both the effectiveness and the efficiency of the sales team to increase revenue. Sales effectiveness includes asking questions like these: Are salespeople targeting the right prospects? Are they promoting and selling the right products/services to take advantage of the organization's capacity or delivery capabilities? Does the organization have good sales funnel information? If not, does the customer relationship management system need to be modified in any way?

Sales efficiency is more geared to managing the cost to acquire or keep customers. This could focus on reducing the sales cycle, realigning, or reducing the number of sales territories, shifting the mix between field and support personnel. Advances in virtual technologies have had a big impact on what is possible in this area. Sales efficiency could also just simply focus on reducing nonselling time like administration.

If pricing is being targeted, what does this mean? Increase in base pricing or reduce discounting? Target specific customer segments? Is the plan to impact pricing decision-making? If so, does that mean modifying the parameters around who has the authority? What are the organizational implications? Will this affect sales incentive plans?

Pricing changes often require a rethinking of organizational policies and related decision-making. These are sensitive areas and take time to figure out. Significant thought must go into how to introduce these changes to a customer base. All these things impact the sales cycle and the timing of when the organization will realize improvement.

COST-BASED INITIATIVES

Cost-based initiatives tend to focus on process or overhead efficiencies. The assessment often identifies potential opportunity to reduce financial line items such as material or labor costs, but the Results Strategy needs to define what that means.

Process Efficiency

Process efficiency initiatives can be defined by functional areas like hospital emergency departments or by larger work streams like patient flow (through the entire hospital stay).

An initiative focused on process efficiency is designed to reduce costs through better operating practices. The basic idea is to produce the same volume with less cost or to produce more volume with the same cost. For each targeted improvement, the strategy needs to be clear on how it will happen and what complications might occur.

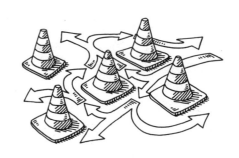

For materials, this might include reducing parts complexity or managing material yield (reducing material lost through the process in one way or another). Or it might be more focused on procurement activities. Like sales, procurement has both an efficiency and an effectiveness component to it. Procurement operating costs are reduced through more efficient operating practices, and pricing is improved through more effective sourcing and negotiation methods.

On the efficiency side, is the plan to improve methods such as ordering practices? Does this require any technology changes? Is the right organization in place? How distributed is the purchasing function? Can purchasing be consolidated across divisions or across functions?

In terms of effectiveness, if the strategy is to improve vendor management to reduce unit costs, how will this happen? Is there an opportunity to improve leverage by consolidating suppliers? Should alternate sources be developed for either leverage or risk management? Is the plan to renegotiate supplier contracts or terms? How will existing inventories or supplier contracts impact timing? Are there any supply chain constraints to be considered?

The strategy needs to identify whether there are any organizational constraints to the improvements envisioned. Procurement effectiveness could include cross-functional development of new products or services to optimize design and costs. If this is envisioned, 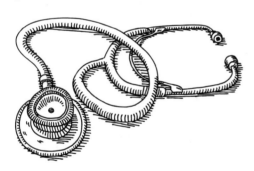 are new skills required? Will targeted changes impact any existing organizational control points?

Sometimes procurement acts more like an administration function rather than a buying function. Changing that can introduce conflict and surface skills issues.

We did a procurement project for a hospital system to reduce the proliferation of parts and materials required by surgeons. The assessment established that there was significant opportunity to consolidate specific items that were virtually identical in terms of functionality but that had varying price points. The current practice was for physicians to make their own buying decisions based on personal preference. As a result, the physicians were regularly canvassed by pharmaceutical companies and had long-running relationships with them.

The most difficult part of the project was not determining the relative efficacy of the parts or materials; instead, it was shifting some of the decision-making from the physicians to the procurement office.

For labor efficiency, it could mean simplifying the process, reducing overtime, or changing the shift structure. Labor is a sensitive area in most  organizations for obvious reasons. It's also one of the more compressible costs. Organizations can reduce labor costs relatively quickly in relation to how volumes are fluctuating.

If the plan is to reduce labor costs, how will that happen? If it means reducing shifts or work hours, are there any restrictions, union or otherwise? Will anyone be laid off, or will payroll be reduced through attrition (e.g., by not hiring when positions open)?

If the plan is by attrition, what are the current attrition rates, and how does this impact the project timing for realizing results?

Overhead Efficiency

Overhead functions, like finance or information technology (IT), also need to be viewed from an efficiency and effectiveness perspective. If the Results Strategy is designed to improve these areas, it must be clear what the performance objective is. Improving productivity in the receivables department might be less important than improving collections.

Strategies in these areas should start with the purpose and the value they bring to the organization and try to optimize that first.

From an efficiency point of view, finance areas are often staffed to be able to manage peak workloads, which sometimes leads to them being overstaffed. The strategy would be to identify how workloads can be moved from peak periods and rebalanced to lower overall resource requirements.

IT departments often have different subfunctions that have different types of workloads. Some are activity-based and some are project-based. Activity-based areas should focus on workflow and capacity management.

A key part of any improvement strategy with a group that is project-based is to understand what backlogs exist, how they might be whittled down, and what, if any, impact on cost this would have.

CAPITAL-BASED INITIATIVES

If a company is trying to improve its capital efficiency, it's usually focused on improving its cash position, or it's looking at specific assets to determine whether they are required or can be reconfigured. The general focus areas that are typical of these projects include supply chain optimization, inventory management, and working capital efficiency.

Initiatives targeting an improvement in working capital tend to focus on reducing the cash cycle. If the objective is to reduce the order cycle time, the strategy should identify what control points (e.g., invoice accuracy) are targeted for improvement and which functional departments will need to be involved.

Inventory initiatives typically target slow-moving or obsolete stock levels, or they're part of a larger supply chain redesign. For initiatives focusing on reducing inventory levels, the strategy needs to understand the implications for balance sheet adjustments and potential issues with the sales group if it means past customers can no longer get legacy parts.

If it's part of a larger supply chain management focus, there are different types of inventories and different functions involved. The strategy needs to discuss how different stakeholders will be involved in the redesign process.

DETERMINE HOW TO MEASURE RESULTS

MAKE SURE SAVINGS ARE REAL

Financial managers are often skeptical when they hear people claim that their projects will generate substantial financial benefit. Many have heard the hopeful promises before and have been disappointed in the end.

Organizations typically have a long legacy of projects or investments that were based on some type of lofty return on investment (ROI), but it's often hard to find a proper financial reconciliation. It sometimes seems like the ROI 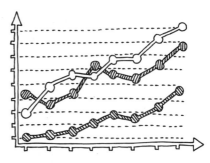 was designed for the initial decision to proceed, not for ongoing management or accountability.

There are several reasons why improvement projects fail to impact financial results. Understanding these reasons helps to avoid making similar mistakes. Three of the more common ones are:

- Squeezing the balloon

- Missing the constraint

- Using the wrong base

One of the heartbreaks of performance improvement is to generate legitimate gains in productivity only to discover they've had no material impact on financial results.

This happens when a productivity gain in one area is offset by a productivity loss in another. The analogy often used is called squeezing the balloon. You generate savings in one functional area, but if resources are simply shifted to another functional area, there is no net improvement.

There's nothing wrong with this if it's an actual strategy.

We were working for Yale New Haven Health, and they were developing a children's hospital. They engaged us to improve the productivity of one facility so that they could move some of their staff to help start up the new hospital.

Sometimes you improve the productivity of a function but all you really do is shift the cost to another department.

For example, you reduce labor in one area but simply move the people to another department. Or you improve the productivity of a production department by having longer runs and fewer changeovers, but this increases inventory costs. Or you increase the number of calls your sales force makes, but they sell to the wrong types of customers or they sell the wrong products or services, causing problems in your ability to supply.

Another example is when you centralize activities to consolidate work, but sufficient costs don't come out of the decentralized locations.

> **Sometimes you improve the productivity of a function but all you really do is shift the cost to another department.**

A common reason for not realizing true financial gains comes from improving productivity of a relatively unimportant part of a function's process. A part of the process that has little or nothing to do with overall output.

In an overly simplistic example, it's like moving a printer closer to your desk. People sometimes make the mistake of taking the minutes you save walking to the printer and multiplying that by some cost per minute to determine a savings. The process change may save you some time, but it won't show up on the financials because no actual cost has been removed.

There are also a few functions in an organization where it's simply tough to move the financial meter. For example, you might produce more but your base costs don't change. So productivity, measured from a financial perspective, doesn't improve. In fact, material or supply costs could increase, so better productivity could end up costing you more.

One example is where there is a high backlog of work. This happens in maintenance, engineering, information technology, and other proj-ect-based functions. Here  you can make changes to improve productivity, which allows you to draw down the backlog and maybe improve service, but you don't reduce any actual costs.

GET THE BASELINE RIGHT

There are several techniques to measure improvement. One basic method is to compare the current period to a similar period in the recent past. Improvement evaluations attempt to demonstrate that relative performance has improved from one period over another. However, relative performance is hard to define.

There are many variables that come into play that both positively and negatively affect results. Some businesses are seasonal, like hotels or retailers. Comparing one period to another in any business can also be impacted by changes in the product or service mix or by changes in supplier prices or employee wages.

In even more practical terms, companies make changes all the time that impact the comparison. For example, hotels undergo reno-vations that change the footprint of the banquet space, manufactur-ers purchase updated machinery, and hospitals adopt new imaging technologies.

The more volumes fluctuate, the harder it is to create a useful baseline—and the more important it is to find reasonably comparative periods. If you use an annual base in a highly variable environment, you look like a hero when the volumes are high, but when the volumes drop, which they inevitably do, you don't look like a hero anymore.

Using averages can be misleading. Averages can be helpful for many things, but you need to be careful about understanding what the numbers are or aren't telling you in a baseline period.

"A person can drown while crossing a stream with an average depth of six inches." There's some debate as to who said this, but it fairly sums up the basic problem with averages: They often hide what 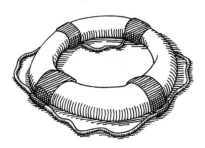 you need to know. They're simple to calculate and an easy way of determining past performance, but they hide variation.

For example, over some prior period, a performance level could have started at 50 percent and ended up at 70 percent. Simple math determines the average to be 60 percent, so 60 percent is now used as a baseline against which to measure future performance.

If the next performance level achieved is 65 percent, you might conclude that performance has improved, which it has over the baseline, but in fact it has degraded from the true starting point of 70 percent.

Using existing budgets to measure results can be effective, particularly because they're part of an ongoing financial system, not a stand-alone evaluation. However, some level of improvement is often already built into the budget, even if it's not always explicit. So you need to be clear on whether the budget reflects the historical base period or budgeted expectations.

Despite the inherent difficulties, improvement evaluations are critically important for managing performance improvement. It forces you to reconcile claimed improvement with actual financial results and creates ongoing accountability.

One of the reasons internal performance improvement groups tend to get downsized when times are tough is that they often claim financial improvement but fail to reconcile that improvement in financial statements. Without that reconciliation, they eventually become just another overhead expenditure and a fairly easy cost-reduction target.

REVIEW THE LINK TO INCENTIVES

Compensation incentives have a powerful influence on people's behaviors, and organizations are often reluctant to tamper with them

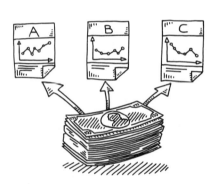

due to the turmoil this causes. Because these systems are designed to influence behaviors in some way, you need to be sure the desired behaviors align.

The trouble with relying on compensation to drive behavior is that it works only if the person sees a direct correlation between the incentive reward and the behavior. The further the consequence is from the direct behavior, the less influence it has.

For incentives to be effective, the expectations and measurement must be very clear so that people understand the way decisions are made. People tend to be accepting and even collectively supportive if the criteria and measurement are reasonably fair. Without this, rewards can easily backfire.

Which, of course, we learned the hard way.

In our own organization, we came up with the idea that random financial rewards would be a novel way to recognize people's performance and to incentivize others. To make it more interesting and colorful, we decided to give out the money in unique ways.

The first recipient was a long-term manager who had done a great job with one of our manufacturing accounts. We bought a silver attaché case and filled it with money.

It turned out that quite a lot of money didn't look like very much when you put it in a briefcase, so we went back to the bank for smaller denominations and then layered the money with cut newspaper underneath. It looked impressive when we were finished.

We invited the manager to dinner and then asked him to come out to the parking lot, where a rental car was parked. We gave him the keys and asked him to open the trunk and remove the briefcase. He wasn't exactly sure what was going on and was a little reluctant to open the briefcase. When he did open it and saw all the money, he was thrilled.

The second (and last) recipient was a consultant who had done a project in a hospital laundry—not a particularly pleasant place to work. He did a tremendous job for the hospital and never complained about the difficult conditions. We gave him his award money in a hospital laundry bag with his initials on it. He was also thrilled.

What we didn't anticipate was the reaction of everyone else in the company. No one was thrilled. A few people were mildly amused by the theatrics, but the general response to both events was distinctly negative. The basic question most people had was this: "What specifically did these two do to deserve this type of reward?" The selection choice seemed arbitrary, and it isolated individuals when they were clearly part of a larger team effort.

Some organizations do manage to introduce creative modifications to incentive systems that support the change program.

One effective approach is to make sure planned improvements correlate directly with operating budgets. Changing budgets midstream is not always well received, as it usually means realigning operating budgets with reforecast performance objectives.

However, doing this serves the purpose of putting tangible meaning into new objectives. It ensures that operating managers have a clear understanding of what is expected and that they actively engage in the change program.

DEVELOP A COMMUNICATION STRATEGY

The purpose of the communication strategy is to keep people informed and to ensure that proper accountability is built into the process for the appropriate stakeholders.

Initiatives go sideways quickly if communication isn't managed carefully.

Many people are affected in a change program, both positively and negatively. A good portion begin change initiatives with a fair degree of skepticism. Many have seen similar programs come and go in the past with little material benefit.

That feeling doesn't go away easily, so you need to minimize people's apprehensions. Letting people know clearly what is going on, and what to expect, helps alleviate a few of those concerns.

STAKEHOLDER COMMUNICATION

The communication strategy to relevant stakeholders, leaders at all levels, functional managers, and employees must be carefully thought through. With so many interfunctional connections within an organization, it's easy to overlook important players. That is a critical mistake.

Projects are usually established with an executive steering committee or a project management office. To drive results, you must determine which executives need to be involved to ensure both functional coverage and timely decision-making. You also need to  develop an appropriate meeting structure and cadence so that you're able to lock down time in what are typically busy calendars.

The project team members must be clarified, and they often shift through different phases of the project. All involved departments or functional areas should be represented as appropriate to the project plan. Team members should have some authority on functional action plans, again to ensure timely decision-making.

The project team meeting plan and cadence must be established. Having a standard agenda ensures that people come prepared for the meetings. The agenda we've found most successful is: results, schedule, people. Results identifies attainment to the plan, schedule talks about what is planned over the near term, and people discusses whether support is required from the individuals involved.

For each functional department or employee group, there needs to be a formal communication plan. The plan should outline what the communication will be, when it should occur, who should be communicated to, and how it will occur.

EMPLOYEE ENGAGEMENT

How employee engagement will be managed throughout the project should also be outlined. Some thought should be put into which employees or employee groups will be most affected by the changes, what the anticipated reaction might be, and what information should be shared.

The most effective way to communicate to employees should also be identified. Some employees will naturally be involved in the actual project process, but there should be a more formal, consistent way to communicate to others. This could occur through town hall meetings, newsletters, or other typical means of communication.

PART 2

WHAT TO IMPROVE

WHERE TO LOOK

The Results Equation

Assess the Opportunity

Create a Results Strategy

WHAT TO IMPROVE

IMPROVE PROCESSES

Align Performance

Develop People

HOW TO GET RESULTS

Focus the Effort

Prepare for Change

Implement Change

CHAPTER 4: IMPROVE PROCESSES

Mindset Principle: Increase Wrench Time

This chapter looks at why process challenges exist, how to identify them, and how to fix some of them.

Why Do Process Challenges Exist?

- Can't fix external problems

- Experience gets in the way

- The way organizations are designed

How Do You Identify Process Challenges?

- Look externally

- Define the process

- Analyze the process

- Observe the constraint areas

How Do You Improve a Process?

- Understand the real problem

- Innovate the process

- Attack the nonproductive time first

- Involve employees

CHAPTER 4

IMPROVE PROCESSES

A fool-proof method for sculpting an elephant: First, get a huge block of marble, then chip away everything that doesn't look like an elephant.

—GEORGE BERNARD SHAW

Although the bulk of our consulting work is now in service environments, when we first started, we worked primarily for manufacturing and distribution firms due to the background and experience of the founders. In the late 1990s, one of our business development people called the Ritz-Carlton Hotel Company and managed to get through to the legendary Horst Schulze, who passed the call over to the head of quality, a gentleman named Pat Mene.

Our timing wasn't great, as they had just become the only company in the world to win their second Malcolm Baldrige National Quality Award. Pat's initial reaction was, perhaps understandably, outrage.

I got introduced to a very animated Pat over the phone as he was dressing down our sales rep. After spending some time trying to explain our audacity, Pat eventually warmed up to us and our approach. He was intrigued by some work we had recently done with manufacturing production systems at a Boeing plant.

Pat was a pretty lateral thinker, and despite his early misgivings, he determined that we might prove useful to them. He had the insight, or courage, to believe that even an organization like the Ritz-Carlton, known around the world for its service and quality, might learn something from the manufacturing world.

We've subsequently done a lot of work with the Ritz-Carlton over the years and with many of their executives who've gone on to run other leading organizations. What has always struck us as remarkable about this organization and its people is their never-ending quest to improve processes. They win all sorts of accolades and awards but continually examine what they're doing to try to improve the guest experience and the performance of their organization.

In this chapter we'll discuss some of the more common challenges organizations face in trying to optimize processes. These challenges are often hidden from view because of the way performance systems are constructed and by the way people figure out how to work around them.

We'll also discuss how to make processes more effective, or to increase wrench time, the concept we discussed in chapter 1.

WHY DO PROCESS CHALLENGES EXIST?

When we study processes, unless we are observing a highly automated process, there is a good chance a typical observation with an employee will reveal that somewhere between 30 to 40 percent of their workday is not truly productive.

This seems remarkable at face value. It means that roughly three hours of a person's workday is not productive. This doesn't mean that a person isn't working; it just means that what they're doing may not be adding any real value.

Ninety percent of the operating challenges we observe have little to do with how hard someone works. The challenges occur due to lack of material or incorrect information, scheduling issues, delays, and other causes that an employee usually can't fix on their own. In the end they're almost all management challenges, not employee problems.

When we share these findings with clients, the fact that there are some operating challenges buried within most processes never surprises anyone. The magnitude of the loss almost always does. What's somewhat surprising is that this hasn't changed significantly over the last thirty years, despite all the advancements in technology and digital innovation.

So how does all this waste still exist?

One possible answer is that the magnitude goes largely unnoticed. In a classic case of good intentions gone wrong, employees and managers figure out clever ways to work around process issues. The work-arounds eventually become the accepted process and the standard for measuring performance going forward.

Opportunity is frequently hidden from view. This might be particularly true in office environments. It's hard to visually see opportunities in digital work areas. You see a backlog of parts on a production line, but digital processing cloaks similar conditions in an office.

When you ask managers how they could improve their processes, a common response is to add people or to make changes to the equipment or technology rather than to address opportunities that might currently exist. This makes sense, because without the tools and training they need, it's hard for managers to know how to be more productive without adding resources.

CAN'T FIX EXTERNAL PROBLEMS

Many managers do not believe there is significant opportunity to improve. It's partly because they don't see it, but it's also because they think it's largely caused by forces beyond their control.

One of the things that paralyzes some managers is something one of our New York City healthcare clients called the X factor. The X factor means problems that were initiated externally (i.e., outside the department) and are therefore difficult, if not impossible, to fix. An example would be when a work order of some kind arrives with incorrect information, causing the receiving department to have to track down the correct information.

External factors routinely affect performance, but it is often less significant than managers think. To separate myth from reality, when we encounter a problem that is considered unfixable due to X factor conditions, we determine how much of the problem is caused by external factors versus those factors that are within control of local management.

Even with legitimate external factors, there is usually more ability to influence external departments than realized. In the example of orders arriving with incorrect information, simply making sure the originating department gets the appropriate feedback, and providing clear guidance as to what is required, will often lessen the extent of the problem.

EXPERIENCE GETS IN THE WAY

Industry expertise is sometimes needed to solve technical problems, but for general change management, it can be a hindrance. Even our own consultants start to lose objectivity if they work too long within specific industries.

Sometimes opportunities exist, and even flourish, in high-knowledge work environments because managers are *too* experienced. High-knowledge environments are those where employees generally require years of technical education to learn their trade, like engineering, technology, medicine, law, and software development. Because the managers in these areas are often very smart, they assume they should be experts at managing.

What these managers sometimes assume is that seeing opportunity and problem-solving are innate skills and therefore straightforward for a bright person. This is simply not so. It takes a lot of humility to find opportunity as well as specific skills to identify it.

Sometimes managers have tried things in the past that weren't successful, and that experience shuts down their ability to reexamine the current situation.

Sometimes people do things because that's how they were taught and that's how they've always done it. We worked for a metal parts fabricator where every morning the maintenance crew went around the plant  and poured hot water into the drains. No one was sure when the practice started or why it needed to be done.

Eventually it was determined that when the plant was originally built, it was surrounded by open fields, and there had been a mouse problem. But that was twenty years earlier, and the plant was now in the middle of a busy industrial area.

> It takes a lot of humility to find opportunity as well as specific skills to identify it.

There was no longer a mouse problem.

THE WAY ORGANIZATIONS ARE DESIGNED

Another explanation is that process challenges exist due to the way organizations are arranged. The most common approach to organization design is to set up vertical functions like sales, engineering, operations, and distribution. Processes, however, tend to flow horizontally through different functions.

As work, or information, moves through a process, certain activities are required to keep the product or information flowing. The activities required at each stage of that workflow, and the associated time of those tasks, vary significantly. A result is that workloads between functions (or steps in the process) become unbalanced, and organizations live with this excess resource capacity buried within the process flow.

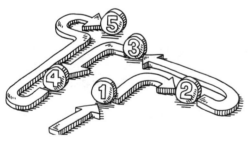

Some project management-based environments try to address this by managing more by process rather than by function. They shift their resources around when and where they're needed. This matrix type of organization is difficult to manage. It's hard to shift resources around because it's not always easy to know when excess capacity is available.

Managers tend to want to keep their people even in slower periods, anticipating that volumes will increase and that their people won't be available. Additionally, shifting resources between functions requires increased skill flexibility, and in some unionized environments, labor rules may not allow it.

HOW DO YOU IDENTIFY PROCESS CHALLENGES?

Improving processes is a bit of an art. Sometimes the best ideas come from listening carefully to your customers and employees. Some executives like to benchmark competitors, although there are a couple drawbacks to that approach that we'll discuss. In any case, we'll go through a few techniques to find opportunities in a process.

LOOK EXTERNALLY

Organizations sometimes use their customers to identify process challenges and opportunities. Feedback is provided freely and openly through many digital channels regarding customer and employee satisfaction.

The value of the information is questionable at times. Due to the uncontrolled nature of the feedback, and the general perception that people with an axe to grind are more likely to take the time to comment, managers tend to accept the positive comments and to dismiss the negative ones.

Some organizations more consciously reach out to customers (and employees) to understand where they can improve. Unfortunately, customer surveys don't always provide useful insight. In many customer surveys we've done, companies score well on important attributes with existing customers and even with noncustomers. The problem is that competitors fare well too.

Many companies exist in highly competitive industries, where all the main players are pretty good. When everyone scores similarly on key attributes, it doesn't give you much insight in terms of improving processes.

It's also difficult to make direct correlations between what customers say and what they do. For example, although customers often say that price isn't the most important attribute, if they see all competitors as similar, price often becomes a key decision attribute.

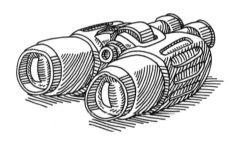 The idea of benchmarking your processes against other divisions, firms, or industries to identify gaps or drive innovation has long been appealing. Unfortunately, it can be very costly, and it often doesn't work very well in practice.

Trying to benchmark a company's processes against other companies (or even divisions) presents three basic problems. First, it's very difficult to define the parameters of a process carefully enough so that you make meaningful comparisons. Second, processes never operate in isolation. To study them, you also need to look at the related management systems and organizational behaviors. And third, because of the first two problems, it's an expensive and time-consuming exercise.

Perhaps the biggest issue is that even if you do overcome the problems mentioned, managers, who ultimately determine whether benchmarking information is useful or not, tend to agree with positive variances and to dismiss negative ones.

Favorable variances reinforce current practices. Negative variances are too easily challenged because the business environments being compared are inevitably different in some way. It's often too easy to use different cultures, systems, people, customers, and facilities to diminish the validity of a benchmarking exercise.

Very often the last comment you hear is the inevitable apples-to-oranges analogy.

Although not ideal for uncovering process opportunities, benchmarking can be useful to identify comparative pricing for similar items, or salary levels for similar functions, or simply to learn from other industries.

DEFINE THE PROCESS

In manufacturing companies, pressures are applied at various stages, from the procurement of raw materials to the delivery of the finished goods to the customer. In service companies, similar pressures are applied from the time a customer makes an order to the point at which the actual service is performed.

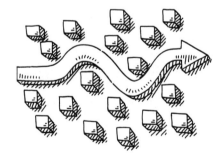

Process challenges are usually observable. In production environments, you see machines jam or workers looking for parts or materials. In service environ-ments, you observe people looking for information or waiting for work from an upstream process. You see challenges in the service provided at restaurants or check-in desks.

To find opportunity, we first define the process itself.

For every focus area we work in, with the help of managers and employees, we create a large wall-size map that illustrates all the steps in the current process, usually by role or function. It is helpful to follow a single customer order through the entire process.[5]

Each of these types of organizations is composed of processes. As we've mentioned, how you define the beginning and the end of any process is sometimes complicated.

For a simple example, we can look at a customer order fulfillment process. At the highest level, an order moves from the sales group to production and then to shipping, as the diagram illustrates.

Process level for Customer Order Fulfillment:

Sales Process	Production Process	Shipping Process

Step level for the Production Process:

Receive Order from Sales	Schedule Order	Order Raw Materials	Produce Components	Assemble Finished Part	Inspect Parts

Activity level for the Schedule Order step:

Check Order Details	Determine Needs	Review Schedule	Determine Priorities	Revise Schedule	Inform Production

You break down the production process into the steps that reflect how value is created for customers (receive order, schedule order, order raw material, etc.). These steps and handoffs are usually the level we need to define when we're doing any process analysis.

The lowest process level is an activity level. Each step is broken down into specific activities that people, or machines, do. In this

5   Benson P. Shapiro, V. Kasturi Rangan, and John Sviokla, "Staple Yourself to an Order," *Harvard Business Review*, July–August 2004, https://hbr.org/2004/07/staple-yourself-to-an-order.

example, the "schedule order" step is broken down into a series of related activities (check order details, determine needs, etc.). This is the level that is generally used for detailed workload analysis and for skills training.

One of the benefits of analyzing processes in this way is that you sometimes find duplicated effort. Duplicated effort is when two (or more) people within an organization effectively do the same thing but at different stages of a process. This kind of wasted effort often goes unnoticed, particularly when the activities are done in different functions.

One example that we see fairly often in a wide variety of industries revolves around forecasting. At one client site, we found as many as seven different forecasts being used by various departments to manage their staffing complements. It's usually related to how much one department trusts the forecasts provided by another department. Sales, finance, production, and procurement often have different vantage points.

Here are a few more common examples of where departments within organizations duplicate effort:

- Multiple handling, due to nonintegrated systems

- Multiple same-company entries in customer databases

- Checking and cross-checking customer or supplier information

- Marketing/selling to the same customers

- Multiple meetings tackling the same issue

- Management reports that contain largely the same information

Some organizations implement knowledge or best practice libraries to try to minimize duplication. However, like most IT-based systems, libraries are only valuable if they are accessible and easy to use and if information is kept up to date. Ironically, they sometimes cause duplicated effort themselves.

One of the best places to look for opportunity is to ask employees. Problems creep naturally into any process, and over time they accumulate. Employees who must deal with them every day are a great source for ideas about what could change.

We give the employees a red pen and invite them to critique the process. "What would you change if you could?" Before long the map looks like some type of contemporary art, with varying sizes and styles of critical red comments. It's the same every time.

As you can imagine, we get to hear a lot of jokes about consultants. One that never seems to get old is "Consultants take your watch, tell you what time it is, and then keep your watch." It's funny, and like most jokes, it's at least partially true.

There is never a shortage of good ideas in the companies where we work, and we go to great lengths to find them by talking to managers and employees. So you might wonder, if all these good ideas exist, why don't companies just use them? The problem is not that there's a shortage of ideas; it's that there are too many.

The real challenge is the time it takes to sift through those ideas to determine how to practically make the change happen and to identify what impacts it would have. In an example of the Pareto Principle, which suggests that 80 percent of consequences come from 20 percent of causes, we usually end up focusing on a relatively small portion of the ideas people identify.

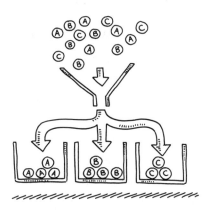

So yes, we often look at someone's watch and tell them the time, but the joke goes too far when it comes to keeping the watch. That rarely happens.

One caution with this technique is that if you ask people for their ideas and insights, you heighten two key expectations. The first is that people now expect that something is going to be done to solve their problems. The second is that because you asked them for their ideas, they expect to be kept informed. It's sometimes easy in the heat of a project to forget this reciprocal obligation.

ANALYZE THE PROCESS

People often don't really *analyze* a process: They create a wall map of activities, but they don't look at the detail hidden in volumes, capacities, and variation. Sometimes the mapped process reflects what people think *should* happen as opposed to what *actually* happens.

Even if the process is well documented, determining the limiting constraints of the process requires understanding the capacities at each stage. Those capacities can vary by product or service, shift, operator, or machine. Analysis requires digging below the surface to get at the core issues.

To start, you need to understand the different streams of work and the volumes and capacity constraints for each key step.

Most processes can be analyzed through data that is generated at various stages of the process. Like the improvement ideas that come from employees, the problem is often not a lack of data but too much data. Also, the accuracy and consistency of the data can vary, as definitions and classifications may differ in various parts of the operation.

Every process has constraints, or bottleneck areas. These areas govern the rate at which you process things. The key constraint is the part of the process that has the lowest processing capability, and it's where work tends to bottleneck.

It's often easier to find constraints in production plants than it is in office environments. In plants, you see where work is backing up. In office environments, you need to analyze the flow of work digitally to determine where the backlogs are growing.

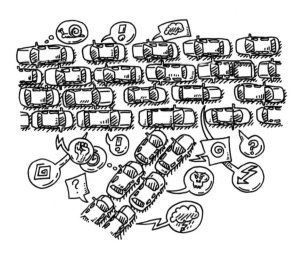

The key constraint governs the processing rate of the entire process. If you increase the flow of work through this limiting area, you increase the capability of the process. Conversely, you can spend a lot of time on nonconstraint parts of a process but end up having little or no impact on the total throughput.

For many process improvement advocates, the ideal workflow is something called single or one-piece flow, where work moves through a process in a continuous flow without any batch processing (or work-in-process inventory). Toyota's production system is well known for this type of workflow. It's not ideal for all environments because it usually requires large volumes, minimal process variation, rapid changeover capability, and very high equipment uptime.

In many cases, processes are more disconnected and move from function to function in batches. Performance loss occurs in these batch-and-queue environments when one operation feeds work or information to another operation at a rate that's either faster or slower than required to optimize throughput.

If the rate is faster, the work backlogs and the operation is a constraint. If the rate is too slow, then the operation suffers from downtime as it waits for the feed or must slow its pace to match the feed. Even in relatively balanced process flows, high error rates at any stage of the process cause this mismatch problem.

One way to uncover these mismatched capacities is to split a larger process into appropriate sections, or subprocesses, and then to determine the processing capacity of each subsection. Sometimes this is obvious, and the sections can be identified by looking for material or information handoffs. Sometimes it's harder to determine, as work is processed, filed, or put away and then returned to by the same person, or operation, so there is no obvious handoff.

The effort to unravel capacity imbalances is often worth it. Smoothing out workflows, even in batch environments, significantly improves process productivity and reliability.

OBSERVE THE CONSTRAINT AREAS

Once we have a handle on the process, we conduct process studies to better understand the constraint areas. Process studies can be any number of methods used to gather insight into what happens during the day, such as in-person observations, remote visual capture, and various means of data mining.

Process studies quantify whether a process is up or down. The uptime is the productive part of a process where value is added. This is the wrench time. The downtime is the unproductive time, where no value is added.

Some of the more common process problems include the following:

Rework	• Doing the same activity more than once.
Process steps not needed	• The same activity is performed in separate areas. • Creating reports that no one uses. • Unnecessary checks made of historically accurate information. • The needs of a business have changed.
Layout of the area	• More physical work or handling of materials than necessary. • Too many people need to work in the same area at the same time. • Too many people need to use the same equipment at the same time. • Poor lighting, inappropriate temperatures, or obstructive noise levels. • Lack of organization that leads to looking for materials, tools, etc.
Equipment failure	• Mechanical breakdowns. • Unplanned variances in the performance of the equipment. • The equipment can't do what it's designed to do.

If you can't see opportunity in a process, it usually doesn't mean it isn't there. It just means you can't find it. If you observe the same task performed twenty times, the time to complete each task may vary substantially. A useful technique is to study the variances.

One of our clients once told us that the key to understanding what drives performance is not to exclude outliers but to study them. By looking at the best and worst months over the last year, he learned what impacted his results.

In one retail sales project we did for a shoe manufacturer, we observed the company's most and least successful salespeople. We studied what they said and how they interacted with prospective buyers.

We found that the simple act of getting people to try on shoes had a marked impact on their likelihood to purchase. The sales reps couldn't specifically articulate it, but their greeting, questions, and even movements were designed to  get you to put on shoes. Over time they intuitively learned that once a person invested time and energy into that action, it led to better odds of making a sale.

Another technique to identify performance gaps, particularly for repetitive activities like processing claims, is to figure out the cycle time for one complete process without any problems occurring.

You do that by determining a theoretical output and then comparing that output to what typically occurs (which is almost invariably less). The challenge is to understand what's causing the variance between the two numbers.

HOW DO YOU IMPROVE A PROCESS?

The overall objective for improving processes is to minimize the inputs, maximize the outputs, and reduce the total cycle time. The basic approach is to either rethink the process itself or reduce some of the waste that occurs through the process.

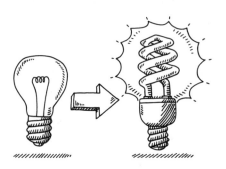

Improving either the productive (wrench time) or the nonproductive components of a process requires different types of problem-solving. Improvements to wrench time require changing the process design.

This was called reengineering until that term fell out of favor; it is now more popularly referred to as innovation. Improvements to nonproductive time require eliminating or reducing waste. This is where Six Sigma, Lean, and their numerous variants are commonly applied.

> The overall objective for improving processes is to minimize the inputs, maximize the outputs, and reduce the total cycle time.

UNDERSTAND THE REAL PROBLEM

To be good at improving processes, you first need to understand the real problem before implementing a solution.

We made this mistake with an auto parts supplier that made plastic components for a large car manufacturer. They needed to increase the throughput of one of their production lines because the line was losing money.

After studying the line, we helped the company implement several method changes, resulting in a 30 percent increase in throughput. The client was thrilled, at least until the financial results started getting worse, not better. A thorough financial review subsequently determined that the company lost money on each part it shipped, so increasing throughput simply made them lose more money faster.

Productivity was part of the problem but not the most significant part. The real problem was a currency exchange issue. The supplier paid most of its costs in one currency and was compensated in another. The exchange rates had fluctuated significantly since the contract was first awarded, eliminating what were already thin margins.

Had we better understood the nature of this problem from the outset, it would have changed the focus of our analysis and better addressed the complexity of the problem.

On another occasion at a food processing company, one of our consultants spent three hours watching a production line, trying to find opportunity. It was a simple quality inspection area, where the product flowed in a continuous stream past trained inspectors.

The consultant noticed that each inspector used a different select-pick-inspect-replace technique and determined that there must be a best practice. He discussed the finding with our project manager. The manager said simply, "I think you have a solution in search of a problem. You'll have more success if you start the other way around."

It's sometimes a mistake to assume that applying a single best practice technique will improve either quality or productivity. In many industries and in many functions, we observe jobs that are done differently by different people. For example, hotel room attendants have the same outcome (a clean room) but often perform the room-cleaning task in a variety of different ways (different order, sequence, cleaning techniques, etc.).

Over time we've learned that it's difficult to change this behavior, and the gains are relatively small. Allowing some variation in approach also gives room attendants a certain degree of autonomy.

The opportunity on the production line turned out to have nothing to do with the inspection process. There was no significant difference in either speed or quality based on how the inspection was conducted.

The overall line throughput (and the corresponding productivity of the inspection team) was improved by simply increasing the speed of the line.

INNOVATE THE PROCESS

While both productive and nonproductive time can be improved, it's often harder to fix productive time. Improving the productive component means taking an existing process and reconfiguring it so that it's more effective.

One of our clients, Frank Halliwell, was the chief operating officer of an international container shipping company. He had a reputation for taking over newly acquired companies and making them more successful—no small feat when you consider how common it is for acquisitions to fail. He was the kind of client who would force you to get to the point if you started running on too long.

I had the good fortune to work with him over several years, and I was fascinated by what appeared to be a formula for his merger and takeover success. I asked him if he in fact had a methodology.

He answered rather bluntly, "Yes. I call it product innovation. You have to improve the product in a meaningful way."

The reason, he explained, is that by focusing on the product, they were forced to understand what customers wanted most, how well they delivered those things, and how they differentiated from competitors.

If they could figure out how to tweak the product (or in this case service) and make it better, there were several key benefits:

- It gave the company a fresh platform to market their service offering.

- It gave customers and prospects a reason to take a sales meeting.

- It gave the company's sales force new inspiration and a reason to sell.

- It provided a reason to market internally and to energize the employees.

He hired us to survey his customers and to compare his company's performance against competitors on key attributes that influence buying decisions as well as to determine how easy it would be for customers to switch suppliers.

From this information we identified attributes that were important but not owned by any single competitor. He'd then modify their service offering to capture and own that attribute and then rebuild the company's delivery and marketing around it.

Frank was an ex-consultant, and consultants tend to be contrarians by nature. It's a common characteristic among people attracted to an industry that exists to change things. Contrarians have an innate desire to be skeptical, take opposing viewpoints, and do things differently. Although it's slightly irritating in a social setting, it's helpful when you're trying to improve a process.

A useful tool, particularly if being a contrarian isn't your natural tendency, is a mnemonic known as SCAMPER, developed by Alex Osborn and Bob Eberle.[6] The tool is a problem-solving guide to get you thinking about how you could improve any product or process.

Here is a simple example of some SCAMPER-based questions that are applicable to any process:

- Substitute: Can the service be delivered with less expensive resources?

- Combine: Can you combine positions or functions?

- Adapt: Are there any ideas that can be adapted from other industries?

- Modify: Can the process be modified to make it faster?

- Put to another use: Can the space or equipment be used at other times for other purposes?

- Eliminate: Can some of the process steps be eliminated?

- Rearrange: Can the process be sequenced to make it more effective?

The idea is to think through these questions while you are observing or studying a process. This can be harder than it sounds,

---

6   Bob Eberle, *Scamper: Games for Imagination Development* (Austin: Prufrock Press, 1996).

especially if your brain isn't wired that way. Sometimes you need to force yourself to take a contrarian's viewpoint.

ATTACK THE NONPRODUCTIVE TIME FIRST

Although some people like Frank can creatively redesign a process, you're generally better off trying to maximize the wrench time by reducing the nonproductive time.

Focusing on the nonproductive time is a better place to start for several reasons. Attacking this portion of time means fixing some of the existing problems that you can control. It also means fixing issues that people currently cope with or have to work around.

If you map out a process to reflect its true cycle time, it's often shocking how much of that cycle time is simply waiting. Parts get processed, put in stacks, and then wait for the next step. It's the same thing with information. Someone does something to an order or a piece of information, it gets handed off, and then it waits for the next person to do whatever they need to do.

This is the wrench time concept viewed from a process perspective. If you increase the amount of time that a part or a piece of information is being processed, you will often reduce the total cycle time.

Another technique is to focus on the best performance period. To do that, you examine the historical data and identify when the process was most productive. This creates a best-demonstrated benchmark. It gives you a way to measure the performance gap by calculating what you would have

produced through a period if you had operated consistently at this benchmark level.

Identifying what caused the best-demonstrated performance highlights the circumstances or conditions that need to be recreated on a more regular basis. The advantage of this approach is that managers are striving to replicate something they've already achieved.

A variation of this that is another useful exercise is to compare performance and methods between people and shifts. This was one of the effective techniques in the potash mine. People are creative when they work at the same thing day after day, and often you find methods that are useful to emulate. This type of study allows you to build a playbook of best practices.

INVOLVE EMPLOYEES

Steve Jobs, Apple's celebrated visionary, once said, "Great things in business are never done by one person. They're done by a team of people." To give employees ownership of the changes going on around them, it's important to involve them with redesigning methods or layouts in their work areas. It's also easy to forget sometimes.

We were working for a company that made aircraft landing gear. Their unique claim to fame was that they supplied the landing gear for the *Apollo 15* lunar mission. One of our consultants was working in a parts-finishing area and determined that quite a few of the area flow problems had to do with the way the equipment was laid out.

The workers agreed with him but had not really considered it as an option, due to the perceived expense of moving heavy equipment around. We did the cost/benefit analysis and then discussed it with the general manager (GM). He loved the idea.

Our consultant drew up new floor plans and created colorful diagrams and charts showing how the flow of material would improve. We presented them to the GM. He loved them too. But then he dealt our momentum a crushing (but in hindsight necessary) blow.

"Did the workers have any input into these plans?" he asked. We told him that they agreed with the original findings, and we had reviewed the new design with the supervisor. He pressed us on whether the actual workers had any input. Somewhat sheepishly we admitted that we had not asked for their input into the revised flow plan.

He said, "Some of these guys have worked here for over twenty years. They know more about the flow of work than any of us, and most importantly, they play a critical role in our achieving any gains from the improved flow. If it was your work area, wouldn't you want to feel like you had some input into how it was rearranged?"

So we went back to the area supervisor and, through him, involved the local workers in the new plan. They did come up with a better design, and, importantly, they were very appreciative of the involvement.

The experience reminded us of the importance of involving the people most directly impacted by potential changes. Not only do they often have insightful ideas but also they are far more likely to support the change if they helped to develop it.

WHERE TO LOOK

The Results Equation

Assess the Opportunity

Create a Results Strategy

WHAT TO IMPROVE

Improve Processes

ALIGN PERFORMANCE

Develop People

HOW TO GET RESULTS

Focus the Effort

Prepare for Change

Implement Change

Mindset Principle: Synchronize Leadership

Performance systems are arguably the most important tool for aligning an organization. They translate the CEO's strategy into specific activities and accountabilities. The main challenge is trying to align levels of management that think differently and that have varied planning horizons.

Why Do Performance Systems Get Unaligned?

- Scheduling is often sequencing

- The point of execution is not well managed

- There's too much data available

- Measurement is used for evaluation, not information

How Do You Identify Performance System Challenges?

- Understand the type of performance system

- Map the system

- Identify the gaps

How Do You Align Performance Systems?

- Limit the key performance indicators

- Improve scheduling

- Make performance visible

- Make people accountable

CHAPTER 5

ALIGN PERFORMANCE SYSTEMS

*In the business world, the rearview mirror is
always clearer than the windshield.*

—WARREN BUFFETT

I grew up playing hockey and lacrosse and spent quite a lot of
time in emergency departments as a result. I always thought
golf seemed like a boring sport that took too long. I had no
interest in playing it until I got a job, and my boss was a fanatic.
Much to my surprise, I found it much more challenging and much
more fun than I'd imagined.

It took me a while to figure out the etiquette, which caused
my buddies some frustration
and amusement. It's a strangely
addictive game. Trying to make
par and using the handicap
system to play against others is a
big part of golf's appeal.

Golf's handicap system is a
very clever, well-aligned perfor-

mance system. It provides a game plan with specific standards from which you can measure your efforts against. There are standards for which tees you should play from, how many shots you should take, and how long it should take to play a round. Golf courses use these standards to manage many aspects of their process, including operating hours, facility management, and course maintenance.

However, imagine someone playing golf every day without a scorecard—just walking around the course, hitting the ball toward some distant flag. This is exactly how many people work, every single day.

We often ask frontline employees how they know if they're having a good day at work. Most people will respond with something like, "I have a good day when customers (or my manager or the sales group) aren't giving me a hard time." What is often noticeably absent (especially in office environments) is any reference to a performance number, whether that's adhering to a specific schedule or attaining a productivity level or a service score. People often struggle to define what a good workday is in any way other than anecdotes.

Many people respond well to clear expectations and the ability to measure themselves. They like visual feedback boards that chart their progress throughout the day. It adds some interest to the workday. They enjoy knowing where they stand relative to others. They like being able to have some sense of accomplishment. People get tired of walking around the same golf course every day without a scorecard.

Performance systems not only provide employees with a scorecard but also they're the primary driver of management behaviors that every organization wants: planning, communicating, problem-solving, and innovating. Performance systems give managers the tools to forecast work, plan it, resource it, execute it, and report on it. It's the basis for how they set targets, manage attainment, coach, provide feedback, and drive continuous improvement.

Unfortunately, these systems become disconnected quickly. When that happens, it's hard for any of those desired behaviors to happen. Keeping performance systems aligned and effective—and managers energized and inspired—is ultimately the difficult task of senior management.

> Performance systems give managers the tools to forecast work, plan it, resource it, execute it, and report on it.

In this chapter we'll discuss the common challenges organizations face in trying to build and maintain well-aligned performance systems.

WHY DO PERFORMANCE SYSTEMS GET UNALIGNED?

One of the main challenges with performance systems is that you're trying to align levels of management that think differently. Senior executives have a longer planning horizon and have to think about financial data on a monthly, quarterly, and yearly basis. They need to be concerned about revenue, margins, and working capital.

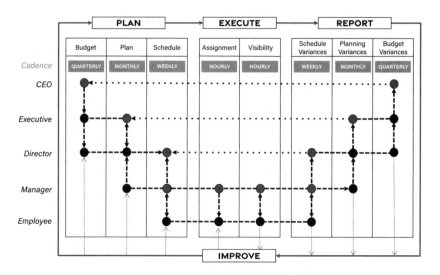

Typical Performance Management System

In the diagram depicting a typical performance management system, you can get a sense of how managers at different levels have different focal points. They overlap at times, but in general they have to worry about different periods of time.

Middle managers deal with a shorter-term planning horizon and work with planning data on a weekly, monthly, and yearly basis. They focus on product or service channels, planning, and operating ratios. Frontline managers have to deal with real time. Their focus is on what is happening today and this week. Their world centers around units, activities, and service metrics. There's a distinct shift from dollars-based thinking at the top to activity-based thinking at the bottom.

Aligning all these different perspectives is difficult for any organization. The way systems try to keep these perspectives in alignment is through conversion ratios. But this is frequently where things get misaligned.

SCHEDULING IS OFTEN SEQUENCING

Effectively scheduling resources to match demand can make the difference between a high- and a low-performing organization. Scheduling is the key control point between the future and the past, between planning and measurement. It's the final setup before execution determines whether you make money or lose money.

In almost every industry we've ever worked in, top clients have taught us how important planning and day-to-day scheduling is for them to manage profitability. Here are a few simple examples:

> **Effectively scheduling resources to match demand can make the difference between a high- and a low-performing organization.**

- Operating rooms: to optimize the use of physicians' time

- MRI diagnostics: to manage equipment utilization

- Aircraft assembly: to match inventory with production flow

- Restaurants: to match staffing with customer demand patterns

- Retail stores: to balance personnel with the ebb and flow of shoppers

- Housekeeping: to coordinate staff with hotel room availability

- Trucking: to optimize loads and frequencies

- Software coding: to optimize resources and manage critical paths

Yet despite its significance, how work is planned or scheduled is one of the least defined aspects of many organizations. It's often difficult to determine how scheduling is accomplished and how few people in an organization fully understand the mechanics.

The result is that organizations often rely on buffers of equipment, people, or time to enable them to properly react to customer demand. It's one of the reasons that large companies, particularly made-to-order-type environments, can be vulnerable to small, nimble firms that focus on a narrow section of the market.

Even though the smaller firms don't have the economies of scale to compete on cost, their focus allows them to reduce the time buffer needed by the larger firms so that they can differentiate on order delivery times.

Scheduling involves taking a forecast of products or services that you are expecting to sell or deliver and then translating it into the resources required to deliver on time. Even from that single sentence, you can appreciate how scheduling frequently goes wrong.

Forecasting demand is notoriously difficult in many industries, and maintaining up-to-date conversion tools (e.g., standards) is one of the biggest weaknesses we see in all organizations, regardless of market or sector.

Schedules are built based on a forecast of some kind. Forecasts provided to operating areas are often inaccurate, or they aren't trusted, so functional managers develop their own versions. Sometimes it's simply because there are different definitions for the key volume indicators that drive the forecasts.

A common problem with inaccurate forecasting is that it results in too many, or too few, people working at any one time based on the volume of work: restaurants, hotels, retail stores, and hospitals are examples of where this happens.

Companies use many different types of software and various technologies to build and to integrate their planning systems. We have seen and worked with most material requirements planning (MRP), enterprise resource planning (ERP), customer relationship management (CRM), supply chain management (SCM), and various other three-letter acronym systems that have been developed.

All these systems are fundamentally scheduling systems. They're designed to help a company match and balance resources to demand. Most of them are cleverly designed and programmed. But as quality guru W. Edwards Deming once observed, "Each system is perfectly designed to give you exactly what you are getting today."

Most of the systems we come across don't operate the way they were intended. These systems rely on the quality of the parameters that underlie the logic of the software. If those parameters don't align with how the process operates, or the parameters aren't managed carefully and kept current, there will be significant disconnects between what the systems advise and what managers believe they need to do.

Where these systems often fail is that they struggle to actually improve scheduling.

Sometimes it's because the software is installed in components. Which components a company decides to install has repercussions on what information is available and how integrated the systems really are.

Sometimes it's because they take too much corrupt data from the old system and move it into the new system. The basic problems we see are often the same: the standards aren't trusted or current, infinite capacity planning is used to cheat the system, planning parameters like supplier lead times are only system defaults, and on it goes.

Another quality guru, Joseph Juran, once said, "Goal setting has traditionally been based on past performance. This practice has tended to perpetuate the sins of the past." Last year's actuals often become this year's plan, effectively building in any problems that were experienced the previous year.

Even when attempts are made to zero base standards, they're often softened by too many buffers so that they better match the current performance level. All this conspires to make it difficult for managers to identify or fix operating problems. It also short-circuits the way they think about how to improve their areas of responsibility.

Without accurate planning parameters, schedules are frequently more a reflection of what has historically happened rather than what will happen. This may be okay if the business is fairly predictable. However, it spells trouble if the product or service offering is complex, or if it becomes more complex over time, or if demand changes significantly.

In these environments, work plans or schedules get revised frequently for various reasons, like customer priorities or equipment availability. If schedules get changed *too* frequently, it results in excessive changeovers and work imbalances. This also leads to work plans becoming little more than exceptions or hot lists, which can negatively affect inventory management.

Often the net result is that schedules are ignored, and the system becomes an expensive data storage of still-corrupt data. Managers end up planning work based on a general sequence of items or tasks, not on an actual schedule.

We spent a lot of time working with Hilton, one of the world's leading hospitality organizations, prior to their IPO with Blackstone. We were brought in by senior leader Patrick Volz to improve operating efficiencies in their company-owned hotels.

Many of these owned hotels were the largest and most complex in their system. To ensure that the methods and results were sustainable, they asked us to work with a software company that had developed a labor management system (LMS) that they were installing across the brand. Pat was particularly insistent that the work schedules produced by the LMS were used by managers to make decisions about staffing. That sounds obvious, but it is quite rare in many organizations, and it is often difficult to achieve.

Pat's fundamental belief was that labor management was a critical element of hotel operations, and with such a large organization, where managers frequently moved between functions and properties, standards and scheduling tools needed to be controlled where possible. He felt the ability to ignore or manipulate work schedules at the local level, which is common with many scheduling systems, negated much of the value of having a planning system.

In hotel environments, parameters such as forecast variability, work standards, minimum staffing levels, labor rules, and shift structures all need to be considered. Planning software that will produce valid work schedules demands rigorous alignment between base assumptions and the practical reality of the environment.

THE POINT OF EXECUTION IS NOT WELL MANAGED

One of the more intriguing things we've learned while working across industries and functional areas is that the actual point where work physically gets done—what we call the point of execution—is often the least managed part of a business or organization.

Managers spend a lot of time planning what needs to happen and then reporting on what did happen but not much time managing where things actually happen.

The trouble with this approach is that things always happen that are not in the plan (information is missing, parts or machines aren't available, etc.). It's not always obvious because employees don't stop working; they work around or bandage the problem as best they can.

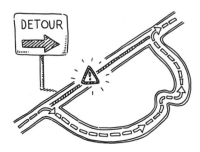

The problems become accepted as part of the workday, and they simply move on and do something else. Managers don't see or know about these problems. Reporting is too long after the fact, so recurring problems eventually become built into the plan, further obscuring them from management.

So why don't managers spend more time at the point of execution? Sometimes it's because there aren't enough useful tools or information available to help managers throughout the day. Missing or lacking execution tools include data control points and visual feedback monitors or boards.

But the main reason goes back to scheduling.

To follow up effectively, a well-thought-out schedule must be in place that outlines where the employee should be throughout the day or week. A schedule needs to be time-based. It needs to identify what is being worked on and when it should be completed. A sequence of activities, or a hot list, tells an employee what to do, but it's not a schedule. It lacks the work-to-time component.

Without that time element, a manager can't identify when there is a variance to the plan. It lacks a meaningful purpose to engage with the employee. It means problems occur without managers knowing about them, which creates waste and rework and frustrates employees.

It causes employees to create the work-arounds discussed earlier, and it effectively turns managers into administrators, expeditors, or problem firefighters.

THERE'S TOO MUCH DATA AVAILABLE

Often managers have too many reports and too much information. Over the past three decades, we've seen a dramatic increase in the capability of organizations to collect and disseminate data to management, in terms of both volume and frequency. But it's often simply too much to process.

Sometimes the problem is distribution lists. Managers often don't need all the information they receive to do their own jobs effectively. Other times it's a self-created issue, because it's easier to create a report than it is to eliminate one. New managers will often create or modify a report for their own purposes, but they're reluctant to kill off existing reports for fear that someone, somewhere, needs the information.

Reports frequently fail to focus on the few key indicators that a manager needs to manage. As consultants, we're sometimes part of the problem: we can become enamored with drilling down into issues and tend to build too many metrics into operating reports.

Over time these things create an obvious problem: there is too much information.

We see a few common challenges with the reports themselves, mostly related to timeliness and purpose. Reports are often too late and after the fact. Managers are busy people, and the longer it takes to get information to them, the less useful the information is. It's hard to backtrack when there are new and present problems and issues that need attention.

Many reports are status reports. They tell a manager the current status of something, but they aren't effective in getting a manager to do anything about it.

Ideally a report highlights a variance to a plan of some kind. The value to the manager is that the variance provides a focus for problem-solving. But if the plan isn't specific and measurable, then the variance loses its usefulness and doesn't trigger any response or action on the part of the manager.

Another issue we often see is that reported performance numbers aren't always real.

Productivity is usually high because performance is measured against inflated standards. The problem with this is an obvious one. If you think you're 98 percent productive, there isn't much room to improve.

There are several other common examples we come across. Schedule attainment is frequently wrong because it's based on output volume and not on the actual product or services scheduled or required. Inventory numbers can be inaccurate due to the way companies cycle count. Lead times are not always updated to reflect actual supplier performance.

Measurement issues can also crop up due to the different time horizons mentioned earlier. Senior leaders focus on lagging indicators, whereas many frontline managers work with leading indicators. Lagging indicators are the outcomes or results of actions taken. Leading indicators are the measurement of actions that are necessary to eventually cause or influence a result.

For example, a senior leader looks at the aggregate sales volumes (either revenue or orders or both), but the sales leader is focused on the number of new proposals bid and won, the number of existing customers retained, or some combination. Challenges occur when the lagging indicators don't align well to the leading indicators.

MEASUREMENT IS USED FOR EVALUATION, NOT INFORMATION

H. James Harrington, a thought leader on process improvement, wrote, "Measurement is the first step that leads to control and eventually to improvement. If you can't measure something, you can't understand it. If you can't understand it, you can't control it. If you can't control it, you can't improve it."

We agree with this concept but with one caveat, measurement should be used to provide information to management, not as a tool to evaluate people.

The performance system, even by its name, seems to imply a control mechanism for managing performance, which it is, but its purpose is to control performance, not people. Measurement systems are most effective if they're used to identify conditions that can be corrected through innovation, coaching, or training.

Measurement should be used to provide information to management, not as a tool to evaluate people.

When measurements are used for evaluation, they cause problems. A British economist, Charles Goodhart, came up with a theory that states, "When a measure becomes a target, it ceases to be a good measure."[7]

The theory suggests that the unintended consequence of measurement is that it eventually corrupts people. There have been a few other insights like this over the years that basically conclude that we can't help ourselves. We'll eventually figure out how to game a system.

One example, called the cobra effect, occurred in Delhi, when India was still under British rule.[8] Local government officials became concerned about the number of deadly cobras running around, so they introduced a bounty for every  killed cobra. It was initially successful but then some clever entrepreneurs started breeding cobras so that they could collect the bounty. When the government learned about it, they ended the program.

That, perhaps predictably, caused the entrepreneurs to end their own program. They released the snakes, which resulted in an increase in the overall cobra population.

We see this sometimes when we follow up with organizations a year or two after a project. The unintended consequence of things like gaming operating budgets is that they disconnect the finance and operating worlds.

When management compensation is linked to budget attainment, there is a natural inclination to limit or manage improvement growth. This makes sense: organizations tend to demand improve-

---

7   "Goodhart's Law," Wikipedia, last modified March 27, 2023, https://en.wikipedia.org/wiki/Goodhart%27s_law.

8   "Perverse Incentive," Wikipedia, last modified March 6, 2023, https://en.wikipedia.org/wiki/Perverse_incentive.

ment every year, so increasing performance too much in any one year is not only tough to achieve but also ensures that subsequent years will be difficult as well.

Here the system tends to reinforce incremental rather than significant change. Also, because budgets are usually based on dollar amounts, the dollars become the focus of management attention rather than the underlying activity drivers that managers need to manage.

HOW DO YOU IDENTIFY PERFORMANCE SYSTEM CHALLENGES?

UNDERSTAND THE TYPE OF PERFORMANCE SYSTEM

There are different types of performance systems that reflect the different types of process environments. The concepts are similar whether it's based on products or services. Each type has certain characteristics that reflect the type of demand, and each type has specific challenges.

Job shops and professional service organizations tend to have low-volume, high-complexity work. They usually require a performance system built around the concepts of project management. These systems need to match demand with resources and require good forecasting, estimating, and backlog management.

Batch or service factory environments are a little easier to anticipate and forecast demand. They're typically a more predictable process with higher volumes. They require good systems for sales targeting, scheduling, and inventory management. The focus for continuous flow operations, or mass service organizations, is on uptime, speed, and throughput.

MAP THE SYSTEM

To assess how well these systems support the different level of leaders and managers, we map it with all the actual documents or tools the manager uses, much like the process map. Then we look to see how useful the tools are and how well the various levels align and search for gaps.

There are three basic types of tools that managers need: planning, execution, and measurement. Planning tools are system elements that support the communication of performance expectations and provide direction. They help managers coordinate resources for planned or expected business requirements. This lets them know what variables need to be monitored and managed. Examples include the following:

- Financial forecasts and budgets

- Labor/equipment plan

- Material/inventory plan

- Job/project planner

- Operations schedule

- Capacity planner

Execution tools help make performance visible during the process. They help managers identify and react to variances as they are happening to keep the area on plan or on schedule. Examples include the following:

- Shift assignment board
- Visibility board
- Project milestone manager
- Downtime tracker
- Quality/safety inspection checklists

Measurement tools track the organization's attainment to the plan and provide visibility and control for the management team. They also help managers learn from past performance so that they can work to improve future performance. Examples include the following:

- Daily/weekly/monthly operating reports
- Variance and downtime reports
- Job cost reconciliation
- Key performance indicator trend reports
- Financial statements

Regular planning, execution, and reporting meetings are another important element of a performance system. When and how often they occur, what they cover, and who's involved all need to be determined and clarified.

IDENTIFY THE GAPS

It's logical to think the place to begin to identify gaps in the performance system is to start at the front end and to review the forecasting and planning parameters. But it turns out, from a practical perspective, it's easier to start in the middle.

The front end may well be the area where most of the actual problems reside, but the way to identify the key issues is to find out what's happening at the point of execution—the point in time when things are made or services are delivered.

If you observe the point of execution, you can see how often schedules are changed and what information (or products or components) are missing or late or are being substituted. Here you also see where buffer inventories are required to maintain the flow. Working backward from the point of execution, you can unravel the root causes of scheduling issues.

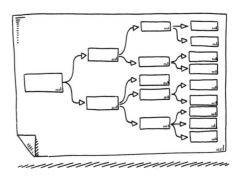

Schedules or work plans can be assessed according to how the base planning standards are used. Planning standards are helpful only if people use them, so a basic question is: Do managers agree with the standards that are used to schedule work?

Another way to look at this is to review the schedules themselves.

- Is there a proper schedule that identifies activities, volumes, and timelines?

- Do the schedules account for factors such as capacity, productivity, and yield?

- Are there any staffing guidelines? Are they based on standards?

- Are the standards current?

Schedules are only as good as the forecast that's used. It's helpful to know if forecast accuracy is measured by product or service streams. Some other questions that can be explored include these:

- What forecasting or statistical techniques are used? Who creates it?

- How are staffing requirements calculated?

- How is work assigned?

- If the area works from a backlog, is the backlog known in terms of work or time?

As you move away from the point of execution, measurement moves further and further away from what's being measured. That's okay and aligns to the roles of different management levels, but it's important that there is a link between what's being measured at each level and what the initial planning parameters were. What links the plan to execution and measurement are the key performance indicators.

Some of the more common performance system challenges include the following:

Forecast Quality	• Forecasts by product or service stream are inaccurate. • Forecasts are in dollars but are not translated into operating units. • Sales forecasts aren't trusted, so functions create their own.
Schedule Reliability	• Planning standards are inconsistent, not used, or considered inaccurate. • The planning system does not generate actual schedules, only sequence lists of things to do or build. • Schedules are changed frequently and at the last minute due to expedited priorities. • Customer change requests are not controlled. • Not enough lead time is provided to stay within schedule, so schedules are altered reactively, changing planned job sequences. • The wrong work is done at the wrong time, causing bottlenecks or limiting output.
Communication Breakdown	• Communication problems among departments occur when requirements aren't clear.

HOW DO YOU ALIGN PERFORMANCE SYSTEMS?

LIMIT THE KEY PERFORMANCE INDICATORS

One of the hardest things about management is knowing what you should be focusing on and identifying the few key indicators that are most important to achieve the objectives. Generally, we find performance systems are most effective when they focus on just three to five key performance indicators.

So the question for any given area is, If there were only three to five indicators, what would they be? A useful technique to identify these key indicators is to speak with leaders at various levels and to understand what information they routinely look at. Through experience, they often learn what to focus on and how to ignore the noise.

Culling a lengthy list of indicators down to the critical few can also help determine what reports and meetings you need or don't need. A manager's time is a valuable commodity in any business or organization. Meetings and reports are time-consuming and cause a surprising amount of time to be wasted or used ineffectively.

IMPROVE SCHEDULING

Improving performance almost always requires better scheduling. Better scheduling almost always means scheduling more aggressively (people, equipment, etc.), which invariably puts pressure on processes and people. A tighter schedule means there is less margin for error.

Completely eliminating scheduling deficiencies is something of a Holy Grail. However, improving the way you schedule usually leads to a better understanding of customer demand, order change management, resource productivity, service requirements, flexibility, and inventory management.

Scheduling systems vary in design and complexity, but there are a few key characteristics that distinguish one from another. Without venturing too far down the scheduling rabbit hole, it's important to understand two things: What is the schedule trying to do, and how does it account for capacity limitations?

Schedules are generated either forward from a starting point or backward from a due date. Forward scheduling is the most common, where the system takes an order of some kind and then schedules each operation that must be completed forward in time. This kind of system predicts the earliest date that an order will be complete.

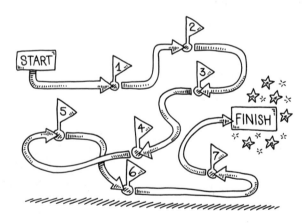

Backward scheduling starts from some date in the future and schedules the required operations in a reverse sequence. The backward schedule tells when an order must be started to be done by the due date.

The second characteristic to understand is how the scheduling system deals with capacities. Scheduling systems use either infinite or finite loading. Infinite loading occurs when work is assigned to a work center based on what is needed over time. No consideration is given to whether there is sufficient capacity at the resources that are required. Finite loading schedules in detail each resource using the setup and run time required by each step.

Schedules usually go wrong when capacities are either incorrect or not considered. It's the same situation with planning parameters like work standards, lead times, safety stock levels, and improper routings.

If you don't address these basic elements, it's very hard to produce a schedule that managers can use. And as we've noted a few times, without a good schedule, it's tough to assign work and to follow up.

As sophisticated technologies such as artificial intelligence (AI) rapidly advance, the potential application of machine learning can be valuable for driving improvement in this area.

With one large multinational service firm, we spent a couple of years helping them develop planning standards for their labor management system. The underlying  technology (which was being developed by another company) was designed to gradually learn how to improve demand forecasting, a critical foundation for their ongoing resource planning. There are many potential applications of this type of automated continuous learning in all aspects of planning systems.

The objective for any work area is to produce a time-based schedule built from accurate standards and planning parameters.

If you can get to this point, schedule attainment should become the most important key indicator for managers. Many of the base operating costs are established when you show up for work in the morning; how productive they are is based on whether you achieve your schedule.

MAKE PERFORMANCE VISIBLE

There's quite a lot of internal debate at our company about where the catchy expression "in the day, for the day" originated. Some claim it was a past client; others say it was one of our project directors; still others claim it is a common idiom that's been around for a while.

Whatever its origin, it's a popular way for us to describe how line managers should think and act. In the day, for the day refers to real-time information about what is happening during the current day, not what happened yesterday or last week. It requires a certain mindfulness or present-moment awareness.

Managers often get performance feedback sometime after an event has occurred, which naturally limits its usefulness. Information that arrives in the day, for the day allows managers to address issues while they are relevant and impacting workflow. There are many benefits, like identifying quality issues before too many products or services have been produced or delivered.

The other subtle benefit of tools that provide information in the day, for the day is that for the tools to be effective, managers must engage with their employees on a regular basis to help correct off-schedule conditions.

This has long-term benefits for both managers and employees and, of course, the productivity of the organization. If you're like us, you may find yourself overusing the expression "in the day, for the day" to the point that it shifts from being catchy to irritating—but it's still useful.

It's also sometimes important to make performance visible to customers.

We were working at a large buffet outlet at a hotel and casino on the Las Vegas Strip. While there was never a shortage of people walking by the restaurant, many saw the lines and were discouraged by what appeared to be lengthy wait times. Managing the flow and capacity of the lineup was related to the revenue potential of the buffet.

According to research, people dread this unoccupied time. It's one of the reasons stores try to hide their lines by wrapping them around corners and place impulse-buy items by the checkout lines.

One useful method change was to post visual signs identifying how long to expect from various points in the line. The posted times gave people a sense of control and were invariably less than what they imagined. Disney, the "universally acknowledged master of applied queuing psychology," takes this concept one step further. It intentionally overestimates the wait times so that its guests are surprised, and even pleased, when the actual wait time is less than they expected.[9]

---

9   Alex Stone, "Why Waiting in Line Is Torture," *New York Times*, August 18, 2012, https://www.nytimes.com/2012/08/19/opinion/sunday/why-waiting-in-line-is-torture.html.

Like the golf analogy at the start of this chapter, making performance visible can be an effective tool for motivating managers, employees, and even customers.

MAKE PEOPLE ACCOUNTABLE

Performance systems take a lot of diligence to make work. The alignment of the system depends on a fair degree of accuracy in the parameters that underlie it. It's easy for things like standards to get ignored when products, services, or processes change.

But if you want effective performance systems, people must be genuinely accountable for at least what they can manage. To help manage that, it's important for an area to have, and to maintain, an accountability matrix.

There have been numerous accountability matrices developed over the years, but the basic RACI matrix is a good method to define ownership and accountability. RACI stands for responsible, accountable, consulted, and informed.[10]

- Responsible: stakeholder(s) who use/interact with the tool

- Accountable: stakeholder(s) who is the owner of the tool and the usefulness/accuracy of its information

- Consulted: stakeholder(s) who need to give input to the decision-making process driven by the information provided by the tool

- Informed: stakeholder(s) who need updates on decisions or progress but who don't need to be formally consulted

---

10　"Responsible Assignment Matrix," Wikipedia, last modified March 26, 2023, https://en.wikipedia.org/wiki/Responsibility_assignment_matrix.

WHERE TO LOOK

The Results Equation

Assess the Opportunity

Create a Results Strategy

WHAT TO IMPROVE

Improve Processes

Align Performance

DEVELOP PEOPLE

HOW TO GET RESULTS

Focus the Effort

Prepare for Change

Implement Change

CHAPTER 6: DEVELOP PEOPLE

Mindset Principle: Develop Dynamic Management

The way that people do things and the way that they interact with one another are the result of years of patterning. To change people's behavior, you need to reshape their environment.

What Are Common People Challenges?

- Productivity is a management problem

- Good intentions have unintended consequences

- Problem-solving is often reactive

- Work assignments are lacking

- Following up is not micromanagement

How Do You Identify People Challenges?

- Experience what the frontline experiences

- Assess manager behaviors

- Observe how people interact

How Do You Change Behaviors?

- Improve manager-employee interaction

- Focus on how managers follow up

- Build a behavior model

DEVELOP PEOPLE

*An employee's motivation is a direct result of the sum
of interactions with his or her manager.*

—DR. BOB NELSON

O ne of our earliest company slogans was "Strategic Productivity." We thought the name was clever because we were trying to sell both strategy and implementation services. We asked one of our advisors at the time for some feedback.

He thought about it for about two seconds and said, "I think you guys have taken two overused words and created a meaningless phrase."

The slogan didn't last very long.

When we went out to pitch our services, we also found that many clients had a good sense of where they wanted to be. They had a strategy, or at least a strategic direction. What they really wanted was help implementing their strategy.

The discussion topic that most resonated with them was this: How do you change people's behaviors?

This started us down the path to being an implementation firm rather than a more typical advisory firm. Having to roll up our sleeves and help organizations implement change forced us to appreciate how difficult it is to get people to change their behaviors. It's one thing to write a report that tells people what they should do; it's quite another thing to get them to do it.

Of the three components of the results equation, people is the hardest one. Analyzing processes and performance systems is, in many ways, an academic exercise. If you put experienced people in a room and ask them to look closely at their processes and systems, they'll figure out better ways to do things.

The hardest thing for organizations to do is to get managers and employees to change their behavior. The way that people do things and the way that they interact are the result of years of patterning. It is very tough to get anyone to change doing things that they're comfortable and familiar with.

One question that sometimes comes up is, Can you change people's behaviors, or do you need to change the people?

We've worked several times over the years with a gentleman named John Timmerman, who's currently the chief operating officer of an acute care teaching hospital. As much as we love working with him, his past training and experience as an Army Ranger makes him one of our more intimidating clients.

When John was working for the Gallup Organization, he invited us to meet with some of their behavioral scientists. He was curious whether either organization could learn from the other, as both were interested in improving management capabilities, but each came at it from a different perspective.

It was a little like nature versus nurture.

Gallup had conducted research and determined that most people aren't natural-born managers, so they lean toward selection and hiring practices as the vehicle to improvement. That was the nature part. Our thesis has always been that you get the management you get due to the environment you create for your managers. That was the nurture part.

It was an interesting and enlightening discussion, and like nature versus nurture, there seemed to be good arguments that it could be either or both. We all agreed that selection is a critical element, both in hiring and in choosing your management team. We also agreed that if you don't fix some of the practical challenges managers face, it's hard to create a high-performance culture over the long term.

While we don't pretend to be clinical experts in human behavior, over the years we've had to learn a few things about dealing with behavioral change. One of the lessons we've learned is that you don't change people's behavior simply by telling them to do something differently; you have to change or reshape their operating environment and then actively support them throughout the process.

WHAT ARE COMMON PEOPLE CHALLENGES?

The most common people challenge we see across industries is how managers interact with their staff. Specifically, how managers assign work and communicate expectations, how they follow up on a work plan, and how they problem solve or innovate their processes.

We also find that it's often the environment that causes people to do things, and they often do things with good intentions. People try to fix the short-term problem, but they don't always appreciate or account for the repercussions down the road.

PRODUCTIVITY IS A MANAGEMENT PROBLEM

One of our consultants did a process study of a mechanic in a large aerospace company. The findings of the study were reported back to senior executives.

One detail of the observations grabbed everyone's attention. Three-quarters of the way through his shift, the mechanic finished his

assignments, so he sat down and read a newspaper. About an hour later, his supervisor showed up and assigned an additional work order.

This finding was heralded as a powerful example of how the company could uncover lost productive time: if they could just get their managers to follow up more often on employees throughout the day.

But this was the wrong conclusion.

It was wrong because it implied that this was an employee problem when it was really a management issue. Here's why the employee was idle: The supervisor had assigned each mechanic what he considered to be a full day's work. The facility was so large (and communications poor in certain areas) that the supervisor required all the mechanics to remain at their final job site of the day so that he could follow up.

The mechanic had done everything he was assigned—he just did it faster than the supervisor estimated. And he remained at the last site, as instructed. Whether he read a newspaper or not was really a moot point.

The real problem was the incorrect time estimation of the work orders and the lack of a backup assignment.

We spend a lot of time watching people work. One of the fascinating things you learn is that problems will happen whether you're standing there or not. The worker usually has little or no personal control over the problem. You also learn that these repetitive and recurring problems eat up a significant portion of an average person's day.

The root problem can reside in some upstream department or area. Somewhere information is missing or incorrect, and this starts a chain of rework or duplicated effort to try to fix the issue. Fixing errors that occur somewhere else in the process is very common in many businesses. If the upstream department needs to change what they're doing, the employee usually can't influence that; only a manager can.

Of course, not all errors originate outside a department. There could be a skills issue, but even if a worker needs training to improve their skills, they need a manager to first recognize that and then to provide the resources or orchestrate the training.

Managers don't have the luxury to stand and watch their employees all day long, so companies build performance systems to help them know when things go off schedule. But if scheduling is flawed, managers can't follow up in a meaningful way. And problems continue to happen.

GOOD INTENTIONS HAVE
UNINTENDED CONSEQUENCES

Improving processes and methods can sometimes have negative impacts on key people within the workforce. A basic objective of many improvement programs is to improve planning. The idea is that if you can plan better, you won't end up scrambling as much when it comes to executing the plan.

Ironically, some people are good at scrambling—so good, in fact, that they are recognized and praised for it. It may even help them get promoted over the years. These are the people who can get things done when you need it.

The trouble is that great scramblers—or firefighters—often fix an immediate problem, but their solution causes other problems further down the line. In many industries you see employees complete a customer's order by borrowing items that were planned for a later order. This creates a problem when the original order is finally processed while the hoarding itself causes a problem by creating artificial inventory requirements.

At one aircraft manufacturer, we did a one-day blitz to retrieve hoarded parts and found millions of dollars' worth of parts inventory stashed throughout the plant. The actions weren't malicious—nobody personally wanted a stock of airplane parts.

In fact, the intent was quite the opposite: People were hoarding to help the process by having parts available in times of shortage. This kind of behavior can, and does, happen in service environments as well.

In hospitals you see nurses keep too many bedsheets and linens on hand because they ran out at some point. This leads to artificially high par stock levels on the floors. You see them order transportation services with too much lead time because they're trying to discharge patients on time, and they've experienced delays in the past. Or they simply don't want their patients to wait. But it leads to poor utilization of transporters and equipment.

None of these actions are done for selfish reasons; they're done to help the patients, or the customers, or the organization.

Great scramblers often have social influence because they are outgoing and action oriented. They can be powerful allies in a change program, but they can also have a strong negative influence if they don't like where changes are leading.

To improve scheduling capability requires significant discipline and accountability throughout the value stream. It's intended to reduce the dependency of off-plan scrambling. It will, in time, have an impact on the workers' environment and individual roles. Some people might be negatively impacted by what, on the surface, looks like a positive change.

We see this with managers as well. It's hard to determine who is a good manager when we first start working with an organization.

Although it's not our role, clients sometimes ask us for our opinion on individual managers.

We're trained to avoid this trap, but even if we had an opinion, we wouldn't be able to share it because we simply don't know. It's very hard to determine who will be eventually good or bad if you change the way an organization works. Some people excel in ordered environments; others prefer some degree of chaos.

PROBLEM-SOLVING IS OFTEN REACTIVE

Like the parts scramblers, some managers climb their way up an organization because of their ability to creatively fix problems. They're often charismatic and have natural leadership tendencies.

Scrambling can become a part of the culture, and good scramblers often end up being managers. So it's not surprising that a common challenge we see with problem-solving is that it's often done in a reactive mode. Something goes wrong, and managers rush to fix it.

The issue here is that often the problem is temporarily patched, not fixed. As a result, the problem will happen again in time.

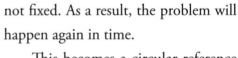

This becomes a circular reference because when a big problem surfaces, managers have no choice but to firefight the issue. If the performance system doesn't properly identify variances, and if managers don't have a decent schedule to identify when variances are occurring, proactive problem-solving doesn't happen.

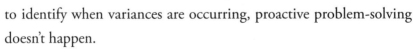

But if you introduce a more structured proactive approach into an organization, some of these individuals can feel disoriented, and it can even affect their social status. They may need to reinvent themselves and acclimatize to a new way of doing things, which is not always easy.

WORK ASSIGNMENTS ARE LACKING

A lot of productivity is lost simply due to how work is assigned—or not assigned. Managers often play the role of a work collator, someone who creates a backlog of tasks. Work is loaded as opposed to assigned. This can be particularly true in knowledge-based work environments. Loading work isn't nearly as effective as assigning work, at least in terms of getting things done productively.

Work backlogs are often in the form of a sequence of tasks or a project list. In these cases, it's the employee who self-assigns the work while the manager follows up on progress periodically. Sometimes this can lead to the wrong work being done at the wrong time because the employee is creating their own work sequence.

When work gets assigned without any related time parameters, it sometimes results in workers pacing. In the late 1950s, Cyril Parkinson published *Parkinson's Law*, arguing that "work expands to fill the time available for its completion."

It suggests that people will change their pace of work based on how much time they have to complete it, which we've observed in various industries and functions. If people are close to completing a task near the end of their day or shift and run the risk of having to either start or be assigned another task, they tend to ease off the throttle.

The fault is not the individuals, however. Stretching work to fill the time allotted has everything to do with assignment and expectations, something a manager controls.

There are several common reasons for a manager to not assign work. Sometimes the employee is experienced and may even understand the task as well as the manager, which may make the manager uncomfortable.

Other times the manager is very knowledgeable but assumes the employee can understand what needs to be done while working at an appropriate pace. However, without clear assignments and follow-up, an employee can run into obstacles that the manager never knows about.

Although work assignment is more common in production environments, it's often assigned without specific time parameters. Employees work off priority or hot lists.

What's often missing is the actual schedule indicating *when* the job needs to be completed. There are many reasons for this, but a frequent culprit is that schedules are changed frequently, often to accommodate rush orders for key customers.

Another challenge with ineffective work assignment is large imbalances in output between individuals doing similar work. Employees' skills and capabilities can vary quite significantly, so it is reasonable to assume that output varies as well.

What we sometimes find, however, is that the variability has less to do with employees' abilities and more to do with how the actual work is assigned.

When work is distributed unevenly, people tend to work at different paces. Some people have more skills or a natural predisposition to work hard at whatever they do. They are the people who managers like to load up with work because they are good at getting things done quickly and efficiently.

However, relying too much on more ambitious workers tends to cause dissatisfaction at both ends of the worker spectrum. Slower workers can feel demotivated while more capable workers can become resentful.

This often results in better workers eventually slowing their pace. This gradual deterioration can be difficult to observe, but it shows up in a measurable decline in productivity over time.[11]

FOLLOWING UP IS NOT MICROMANAGEMENT

If managers don't assign work effectively, they aren't able to follow up systematically. But the whole notion of following up is sometimes misunderstood.

It's not uncommon to hear an industry veteran reflect on their success by saying something like "I was successful because I hired good people and then I got out of their way." It's a good sound bite, and it may work in some circumstances, but it's not great management.

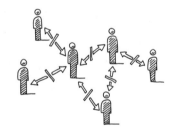

Often managers and employees are not overly comfortable with the concept of following up. Following up with staff at regular intervals is seen by some as micromanaging. It's also viewed by some as the antithesis of employee empowerment. But defining employee empowerment, as some managers do, as a proxy for getting out of their way ignores a key role of a manager.

---

11   Rebecca Knight, "Make Sure Your Team's Workload Is Divided Fairly," *Harvard Business Review*, November 14, 2016, https://hbr.org/2016/11/make-sure-your-teams-workload-is-divided-fairly.

Most operating challenges that impede people's productivity need management intervention to be fixed. Managers need to know what their people are doing and how they are progressing, at least periodically, so that they can help identify when challenges crop up.

It's not a question of getting out of their way; it's a question of what can managers do to help without getting in the way. Employees can most effectively be empowered if managers perceive their own role not as someone who monitors performance but as someone who helps remove obstacles.

> Employees can most effectively be empowered if managers perceive their own role not as someone who monitors performance but as someone who helps remove obstacles.

The notion that follow-up equals micromanagement tends to get worse, not better, in high-knowledge work areas.

We were working with software engineers for a company that provided airports with sophisticated interterminal trams. This company had extended design and development programs underway. The development period would take two years, so hidden problems today could cause significant rework and cost down the road. A key operating concern during the design phase was the timely coordination of coding and testing.

To properly follow up with software engineers, managers needed to break down the projects into smaller, more manageable packages of work (from monthly to weekly). The software engineers viewed this form of work assignment as a proxy for micromanagement and openly resisted the change.

This company required more bottom-up input and feedback to monitor the in-design/development issues to improve processes and to solve technical issues. In their case, the experts were more the hands-on software engineers and not the managers.

The purpose of more frequent follow up was to help the manager better coordinate all the moving parts that existed in the development program. Identifying off-schedule conditions closer to the point where they occurred helped to reduce the frequency of schedule changes and the amount of rework.

HOW DO YOU IDENTIFY PEOPLE CHALLENGES?

EXPERIENCE WHAT THE FRONTLINE EXPERIENCES

The most effective way to identify people challenges is through practical observation. Spending a few hours living through someone else's experiences can be very enlightening. There's no right or wrong for how much time you should spend, but the more time you spend, the more challenges you'll see.

When we introduce the concept of observing processes, whether in person or remote, managers are sometimes concerned that a process study is artificial, because surely a person being observed will be more diligent or more attentive than normal, which could inflate the capability of the process. This turns out to be somewhat irrelevant.

Problems happen whether someone is observing or not. People receive the wrong information, a required part is missing, they need to redo something, a machine breaks down, or they simply must wait for some reason.

Over the years we've had a few less-than-flattering nicknames thrown our way. One of the harsher ones was "Cushman Bait." This was the nickname given to us at an aerospace manufacturing plant. Cushman was the brand name of the utility vehicle employees drove around the plant.

You need pretty thick skin to stay in the consulting business.

This particular plant was unionized, although that's not really relevant, as it's fairly common for workers (unionized or not) to be less than thrilled when we spend time observing the process. Employees sometimes feel that watching them is some kind of Big Brother intrusion and that the outcome won't be beneficial to them. However, what is almost always surprising is how quickly this opinion changes.

By the time we're finished, most employees agree that there is no better way to understand their daily issues than to spend a day in their shoes and to see the world through their eyes, completely unfiltered. It's the best way to understand what they have to deal with on a daily basis.

To help ensure that the observation experience is positive, we follow a few simple guidelines. We take the time to explain that the purpose is to watch the process—not to watch individuals. We share what we're seeing and let them know what we plan to do with the information. We also follow up with them afterward to let them know what was collectively learned.

Some of the more common people-related challenges we come across include the following:

Idle/waiting	• Waiting for inputs, quality, materials, equipment, or assignments. • Each area processes work at different rates, causing imbalances in the flow. • An employee finishes a task and doesn't know what to do next. • Work volumes fluctuate significantly. The manager doesn't level the workflow and eliminate variances by making backup assignments to be accomplished during slack periods or downtime.
Pacing/lack of expectations	• Work pacing (employees pace their work to the amount of time they have) is difficult to identify because there's an appearance of constant activity. • When people have repetitive tasks, the volumes produced through the period vary substantially for no apparent reason. • When managers have not given any expectation of how long the work should take, leaving the employee to dictate the rate of work. • Company policies are ignored (late to work, excessive break times, lunch periods, etc.).
Low-priority work	• Employees run out of work, and if the manager is not around, the employee will do whatever work is available, but it may be of low priority. • Doing work that doesn't need to be done. • Making work assignments that aren't necessary.
Skills gaps	• Employee doesn't know the most effective methods. • Lack of skills training. • Lack of flexibility due to lack of cross-functional training.

ASSESS MANAGER BEHAVIORS

Many managers, our own included, believe that they're better managers than they actually are. Managers aren't alone, however. There's a well-documented psychological bias called the above-average effect, which is the tendency of most people to believe they're above average, despite the obvious mathematical impossibility.[12]

There is a similar and related cognitive bias called the Dunning-Kruger effect.[13] This theory suggests that the less skilled you are at doing something, the more likely you are to overestimate your own performance, precisely because you don't really know how to judge it properly.

In defense of all managers, managing is extremely difficult, regardless of industry, and requires an uncommon blend of skills. Many of us got to where we are due to our technical proficiency, not our management skills. Organization design often works against us, and performance tools don't support us nearly as much as they should. All this creates a tough environment to be a good manager.

Is this a big deal? So management is tough, and our own self-assessments are a little high. It turns out that this matters a lot if you are trying to drive up performance. A key part of most performance improvement efforts is getting managers to change how they interact with their staff: how they set expectations, follow up, and coach. If

12   American Psychological Association, "Above-Average Effect," accessed March 13, 2023, https://dictionary.apa.org/above-average-effect.

13   Kendra Cherry, "What Is the Dunning-Kruger Effect?," Verywell Mind, November 8, 2022, https://www.verywellmind.com/an-overview-of-the-dunning-kruger-effect-4160740.

managers don't see a need to adjust their behaviors, it's very hard to get them to change.

We address this issue by doing what we call management studies. We often spend a full day observing a manager and then break their time into various categories. To compare what they actually do with what they think they do, we ask them at the end of the day to do their own categorization.

Almost invariably managers initially misjudge how they spend their time. Most studies identify that the time a manager meaningfully engages with an employee is less than 10 percent of their day.

> If managers don't see a need to adjust their behaviors, it's very hard to get them to change.

If they don't have good scheduling tools, it's almost impossible to be much higher than that. However, if you ask them what they think they do, most believe they spend 20 percent or more of their time doing this.

That gap needs to be addressed as part of the change process.

OBSERVE HOW PEOPLE INTERACT

We work in many businesses that replicate their information systems and business processes as they grow (e.g., construction companies, wineries, distribution centers). Or they acquire new operations and then migrate them to the way they do things.

To enable this growth, organizations often move their leaders and managers around. Hospitality is an industry where this is very common. The difficulty is that people with experience tend to treat the operating problems they come across as the same ones they've encountered in the past. This isn't necessarily bad. Sometimes problems are similar, and history has a way of repeating itself, but problems are very much context specific.

Despite virtually identical systems and processes, the makeup and style of management can be radically different from one location to another. Multiple locations, doing essentially the same thing, can have very different challenges. Often the biggest single variable is how people interact with one another.

HOW DO YOU CHANGE BEHAVIORS?

IMPROVE MANAGER-EMPLOYEE INTERACTION

Like most of us, managers repeat the same behaviors over many years and those behaviors become deeply entrenched. But to get lasting results, you need managers to change or modify some of those behaviors. When we say that, almost universally executives nod their heads in agreement. But when we all say it, what do we mean? What does changing management behavior actually look like?

There are many ways to categorize management behavior, but most organizations would like their managers to possess the following basic skills:

- Resource planning

- Work scheduling

- Assigning work and communicating expectations

- Following up, giving feedback, and problem-solving

- Training and coaching to improve performance

- General administration

The area we focus on is the time managers spend directly engaged with their staff. We call this interaction dynamic management. Dynamic management is the time managers spend planning, communicating, following up, and proactively problem-solving. To do it well takes courage, commitment, passion, and humility.

DYNAMIC MANAGEMENT

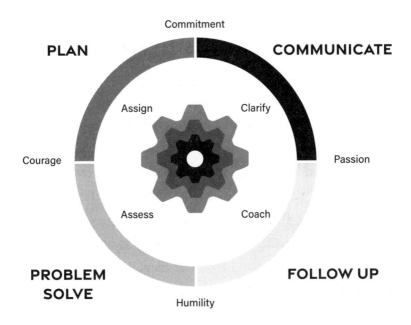

It all sounds basic, but it's extraordinarily difficult to do consistently. It requires all the skills that managers are taught but that are hard to apply in real-life situations, like active listening or understanding how to motivate people who have different social styles.

To get managers to appreciate the need to modify some of their behaviors, they first must properly understand how, and why, they're spending their time currently. With a better understanding of what they're doing, they're more able to rethink how their time might be more effectively distributed and what their new workday might look like. That can be a significant behavioral change for some people.

To achieve this, we repeat the management studies discussed earlier but this time stop whenever we see an issue and briefly discuss what happened. The study itself doesn't change behavior, but it does help to recalibrate people's perceptions.

Another thing that can be picked up doing these management studies is to identify *where* managers spend their time. Many years ago, we started doing a study somewhat unimaginatively called the whereabouts study. The idea was to identify where a manager spends most of their time during the day. We correlate it to what is happening in the business at the same time and determine whether it would be

more useful for the organization to have the manager's day look differently.

In many cases, managers spend a great deal of their time behind closed doors, either in their offices or in meetings. This may be necessary and useful time, but it can also raise several questions related to appropriate roles, span of control, and activity allocation.

We work directly with the manager to determine how their time could be reallocated to support the process and their people more effectively. Managers usually have a full day, so you can't simply assign additional tasks to them. You need to reconfigure their current day.

In most cases, managers understand the basic logic and need for increasing dynamic management. However, physically changing their basic workday from what they are currently doing—to what they ideally should be doing—underscores the need to provide them with different tools and training.

It also requires communicating to team members to ensure they understand why the manager is doing it and what the benefit for them will be.

FOCUS ON HOW MANAGERS FOLLOW UP

We focus on how a manager communicates with an employee to understand whether there are any problems that need intervention. The intervention could be problem-solving, training, coaching, or any combination.

Regular and consistent follow-up is a daunting task for most managers at any level. But to be a useful support, managers need to follow up and find out how someone is doing. Without a proper schedule, managers can't follow up properly.

Even with a proper schedule, if it's not common behavior, and if it's not com- municated properly, it's hard for employees not to assume that the purpose is to  somehow police their productivity. For frontline or newly promoted managers, the social dynamics can be awkward as well.

Training programs often ignore these difficult situations and don't train managers in how to handle them. It's one of the reasons managers go to training courses, get inspired, and then fall back to their old ways when they reenter the harsh reality of their workplace.

The best method to get managers to follow up is to make sure they have the tools they need and the right environment in which to do it effectively. The right environment includes ensuring that employees understand what the manager is trying to do.

If you take the time to explain to employees that the manager's job is to support them, and if you make it a steady, consistent practice, you can overcome many of the anxieties that are initially present. But like any new skill, it takes practice and repetition.

Most people want their work to have purpose, and they enjoy being productive. When managers follow up in a meaningful way, the relationship between manager and employee changes from a reactive orientation to an active mutual collaboration.

If you can get to this point and make it a habit, both managers and employees will be more engaged working together to get things accomplished.

BUILD A BEHAVIOR MODEL

To define what management needs to do to help support employees, it can be effective to build a visual model of behavior that provides

clarity as to what is expected from managers at different levels of the organization.

The model should define how managers assign work, communicate expectations, follow up on the plan, provide feedback, coach, and train. It can define what a typical week, month, or even year might look like.

Every organization and each individual function must tailor their own management profile. Behavior profiles change by industry and company and within companies by their organizational hierarchy and function. How frontline managers allocate their time is naturally different from how executives allocate theirs. Similarly, sales managers and production managers have very different behavior profiles.

Understanding the current and desired profile at each level can be helpful in making sure that the organization is aligned and optimizing its valuable management resources. It's also a useful mechanism for onboarding new managers.

> When managers follow up in a meaningful way, the relationship between manager and employee changes from a reactive orientation to an active mutual collaboration.

Defining this expectation will cycle back to how effectively the performance system provides managers with the appropriate tools.

PART 3

HOW TO GET
RESULTS

WHERE TO LOOK

The Results Equation

Assess the Opportunity

Create a Results Strategy

WHAT TO IMPROVE

Improve Processes

Align Performance

Develop People

HOW TO GET RESULTS

FOCUS THE EFFORT

Prepare for Change

Implement Change

Mindset Principle: Build Ownership

The Focus Meeting is designed to energize the organization and to ensure that operating managers have ownership of the initiative. The purpose is to communicate what's changing, why it's important, and why this will be of benefit to people. The meeting also clarifies what specifically needs to happen, what people need to know, and what they need to do.

Row in the Same Direction

- Understand the emotional cycle of change

- Transfer ownership to operations

- Pre-present ideas

Communicate the Vision

- Articulate what's in it for everyone

- Why selling aspirins, not vitamins, is more effective

- An effective way to present complex change

Avoid the Traps

- Make sure people understand the message

- Forget the platitude to work smarter, not harder

- Appreciate cultural context

- Manage the headlines

- Don't give mixed messages

CHAPTER 7

FOCUS THE EFFORT

The success of a vision is determined by its ownership
by both the leader and the people.

—JOHN C. MAXWELL

We had done quite a lot of work in the transportation industry, and through word of mouth, we were invited to speak at a national convention. We prepared what we thought was an insightful speech that essentially criticized the industry for its lack of differentiation. The title was something like, "Does Anybody Know What Logistics Means?"

In advance of the convention, we shared the presentation with one of our business advisors, who happened to be a well-regarded CEO in the industry. We told him that we thought it would be a good idea to ask the audience some questions throughout the presentation, to make it more interactive.

He listened quietly. Then, when we were finished, he shook his head and said, "You've got to be joking."

Not really intending the speech to be funny, we asked him what he meant.

He said, "Guys, you're talking to people who have successfully built their own businesses, who have paid money to come to a national convention to have fun and maybe learn a few new things. They didn't come to be lectured by consultants. And resist the urge to question them, because you'll be asking them to critique themselves, which they obviously won't want to do."

We thanked him for the input and casually ignored it. At the convention, we somewhat ironically followed a motivational speaker, who we were convinced would bomb. We were wrong about that too.

By the end of the presentation, the mood in the room was electric. He had people shouting and standing on their chairs. There was a feverish buzz in the air, and we were almost trampled as people exited the room, scrambling to buy signed copies of his books.

We walked onstage, and almost immediately the person introducing us mispronounced our company name (another lesson learned). We then started into our academic criticism of the industry, hoping to ride the wave of enthusiasm from the motivational session.

With each point we made about how the profit of the industry was declining because of a lack of differentiation, you could actually feel the excitement of the previous speech drain from the room.

At one point, we put a confusing value proposition up on the screen, ripped straight from the industry leader's website, and asked someone from the audience to comment on it. He politely refused, twice.

Finally, after the third prodding, he explained, "Hey, I work for the company you're using as an example, so it isn't appropriate for me to comment." The awkwardness that followed may be the only thing that anyone remembers from that presentation, including us.

In hindsight, I'm not exactly sure what we were trying to accomplish or why we didn't listen to our advisor. We certainly didn't align our message with the audience. This chapter is about doing a better job of that. (I probably should've asked the motivational speaker to write this chapter.)

ROW IN THE SAME DIRECTION

We have discussed improving three key components of results: process, performance, and people. The output of those efforts is something like a playbook, a road map for how focus areas will improve. But between the playbook and the implementation, you have to get those thoughts and ideas into the collective consciousness of the organization and mobilize people to change.

All executives want their employees to act in ways that support the overall strategic direction of the organization. But how do you get people aligned and rowing in the same direction? Strategic direction and even the concept of alignment can mean very different things to different people. When organizations are not aligned, they struggle to get strategic initiatives accomplished.

One of the more useful alignment models we've seen is the model for managing complex change developed by Dr. Mary Lippitt and expanded by Dr. Timothy Knoster.[14] The model suggests that there are six elements you must align to create effective and lasting change: vision, consensus, skills, incentives, resources, and an action plan. Even missing one of these elements, despite having the others, can be a problem.

LEADING AND MANAGING COMPLEX CHANGE

Vision +	Consensus +	Skills +	Incentives +	Resources +	Action Plan	= Change
	Consensus +	Skills +	Incentives +	Resources +	Action Plan	= Confusion
Vision +		Skills +	Incentives +	Resources +	Action Plan	= Sabotage
Vision +	Consensus +		Incentives +	Resources +	Action Plan	= Anxiety
Vision +	Consensus +	Skills +		Resources +	Action Plan	= Resistance
Vision +	Consensus +	Skills +	Incentives +		Action Plan	= Frustration
Vision +	Consensus +	Skills +	Incentives +	Resources +		= Treadmill

Adapted from Knoster, T. (1991) Presentation in TASH Conference, Washington, D.C.
Adapted by Knoster from Enterprise Group, Ltd.

The model is a useful guide to illustrate the purpose of a key meeting we call the Focus Meeting. The meeting is a presentation that occurs a couple of months into the change initiative and is designed

---

14   Sergio Caredda, "Models: The Lippitt-Knoster Model for Managing Complex Change," Sergiocaredda.com, March 3, 2020, https://sergiocaredda.eu/organisation/tools/models-the-lippitt-knoster-model-for-managing-complex-change.

to communicate the vision, skills, incentives, resources, and action plans needed for effective change.

To achieve success, the meeting must provide a new and credible environment that benefits people. When executed effectively, a Focus Meeting can result in increased consensus.

As the name suggests, the meeting concentrates the thinking of both the project team and the involved managers. During the early stages of an initiative, many excellent ideas are generated, but at some point they must be narrowed down to achievable specifics within a reasonable time frame. The meeting brings everything together.

The meeting also clarifies the role of supporting functions such as finance, information technology, human resources, project management offices, or internal or external consulting support.

UNDERSTAND THE EMOTIONAL CYCLE OF CHANGE

It's helpful to consider the context of where most organizations are at this stage of the initiative. People have seen others reviewing their processes and analyzing activities in their work area. There is uncertainty with what is happening, and the benefits of making changes are not clear at this point.

More than fifty years ago, Don Kelley and Daryl Conner developed a concept they called the emotional cycle of change model, and a modified adaptation is depicted in the following diagram.[15] The cycle identified five stages that people typically go through when dealing with change: uninformed optimism, informed pessimism, hopeful realism, informed optimism, and completion.

---

15   Marcus Cook, "How Founders Should Think about the Emotional Cycle of Change," *Inc.*, November 4, 2021, https://www.inc.com/marcus-cook/how-founders-should-think-about-emotional-cycle-of-change.html.

THE EMOTIONAL CYCLE OF CHANGE
HAS TO BE MANAGED

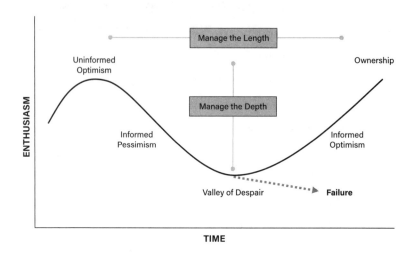

For our purposes, we modified the final stage from completion to ownership to reinforce the notion that change is a journey rather than an event.

The model suggests that people often start an initiative with some excitement because it's new or different, but when they realize how much effort it takes to change, optimism can go south quickly. The Focus Meeting manages the length and depth of this emotional cycle.

Change is a grind for most people, and we all need periodic encouragement to remind us why we're doing things. The Focus Meeting provides that uplift. It communicates the challenges that are holding us back, identifies what we're going to do about it, and presents the results we can expect. When communicated properly it reenergizes everyone involved.

TRANSFER OWNERSHIP TO OPERATIONS

A key purpose of the Focus Meeting is to transfer ownership of the project. The ultimate success of a change initiative requires ownership from affected leaders and managers. Managers in the areas being changed must believe they can improve, participate in generating solutions, and feel there is some benefit to them at the end of the day.

This is not always easy to do. Often there is healthy skepticism, and not all managers buy into the need to change. While you don't need full buy-in, you do need acceptance of where the current performance level is and acknowledgment that there is room for improvement.

For many years we conducted these presentations ourselves while executives and area managers looked on. On one occasion, the day before  the Focus Meeting, we dropped in to see a senior executive at a division of H. J. Heinz and gave him a quick overview of what to expect.

After we finished, he said, "It sounds great, but I don't want you presenting this to me. No offense, but I don't really care what you think. I care about what my managers think. I'd like them to present tomorrow."

We mumbled something like, "Of course" and left the room, trying not to let him see the slight panic in our eyes. We weren't certain we had prepared the managers sufficiently for them to present the meeting. The concern turned out to be unnecessary. The managers embraced the chance to speak for themselves and did a great job presenting.

The client was right; our approach was wrong. It wasn't important what we thought, particularly at that stage in the project. The only thing that mattered was whether managers believed they could improve. From that point forward, client leaders and managers always present the Focus Meeting, and we say very little unless asked.

But managers can't just show up at the meeting and be expected to present the material. They need to be carefully brought along throughout the early developmental weeks to ensure that they believe in what is being presented and that they take ownership of any changes being suggested.

The experience forced us to rethink the front end of our projects to ensure that managers are properly involved and engaged from the outset.

PRE-PRESENT IDEAS

To adequately transfer ownership, all relevant managers need to be aware of what is being presented. Key participants should be familiar with the material and not be surprised with new ideas. By pre-presenting the information, you handle objections on a one-on-one basis and either reach a resolution or modify the method change accordingly.

Almost any new idea or change will be met with a certain amount of resistance from people who are affected. People hate surprises, good or bad, because it can represent a loss of control at best and an embarrassment at worst. If you present to a group and catch someone off guard, that person may react negatively because they feel they have been put on the spot. Their negative reaction can quickly derail the entire meeting. It can also start a cascade of doubt and create apprehension in others present in the room.

Many otherwise good ideas have been torn to shreds in a group meeting where new ideas were presented.

We learned this lesson the hard way at a meeting where we were presenting changes that had been developed with the help of the leaders of the food and beverage areas of a luxury resort. Several changes involved the movement of food to and from the kitchens, so the head chef was invited to the meeting. That was a good idea.

Unfortunately, none of the method changes had been presented to the chef in advance.

That was a bad idea.

The chef objected to most of the method changes that were presented. The objections weren't overly critical, and many in fact had been recognized and dealt with already. But the objections derailed the flow of the meeting, and with each objection the general manager became increasingly uneasy with the level of buy-in of his management team.

A herd mentality started to develop. Objections led to more objections, which led to more discomfort around the room. The positive buy-in from the area managers started  to dissipate. Three-quarters through the allotted meeting time, and less than halfway through the agenda, the GM politely asked us to do more work on selling the method changes and rescheduled the meeting.

People usually fail to pre-present because they don't think anyone will object, or they run out of time. Painful experience usually teaches us to never underestimate how many people dislike surprises.

It's easy to find yourself in the position where you don't have time to review with everyone before the meeting, but good ideas routinely go down in flames because of this error.

COMMUNICATE THE VISION

Communicating the organization's vision, and why improvement is necessary, is one of the more important messages in a change process. Executives know this and often go to great lengths to paint a picture that outlines the need for change.

These messages explain the reason for change and how the organization will be more competitive as a result. But sometimes it can come across as corporate platitudes if it doesn't resonate at an individual level.

Through the front end of any change process, the questions most people have are these: Why are we doing this? Why are we doing this now? And how will this affect me? The Focus Meeting is a chance for leaders of the organization to answer those questions.

> Communicating the organization's vision, and why improvement is necessary, is one of the more important messages in a change process.

A senior leader should kick off the meeting by communicating the vision of the organization. Following the senior leader, managers present information for their respective areas. Backed by visual support, they review the current state as well as the changes needed to get the required results. There are four elements to the presentation:

- Base results

- Current state

- Results Strategy

- Required results (R2)

The base results visually depict the financial and operational performance during the base period. The current state summarizes the assessment that reviewed key elements that create results: process, performance, and people.

The Results Strategy section summarizes the area strategies for improvement. The required results (R2) section is effectively a mirror of the base results section. It illustrates what results are expected and the anticipated timing.

For each project area, the responsible manager explains where the results are going to come from and what specific steps must be done prior to implementation to ensure success. It lets everyone know, at least theoretically, what the new world will look like and what is expected of them.

For each section of the Focus Meeting, it helps if you keep the message simple. There's a lot of research that supports this practice.[16] There are rules of three in many different disciplines, including medicine, aviation, mathematics, and economics. Slogans and book titles are often three words. Jokes, plays, and speeches are often delivered in three parts. Three key points on a particular slide or three key themes in a presentation seem to be the maximum amount you can do before people are either bored or confused.

One of the benefits of using the rule of three is that it forces you to distil, and clarify, your message. Just as it's easier for an audience to absorb, it's also easier for you to communicate.

---

16   Daniel I. Chu, "The Power of Three," Association of Academic Surgery, January 10, 2017, https://www.aasurg.org/blog/the-power-of-three.

ARTICULATE WHAT'S IN IT FOR EVERYONE

Resisting change is apparently part of our survival instincts.

Sociologists believe that change robs us of our sense of control because it presents a new environment or an unfamiliar pattern of behavior. Because we don't like to lose control and favor the predictable over the unpredictable, many of us would never change if we didn't have to.

Few of us seek change for the sake of change. We need some kind of external or internal force that tells us that staying with the current path is more dangerous than trying a new path. Change requires a sense of fear or urgency. In other words, change requires a crisis of some sort.

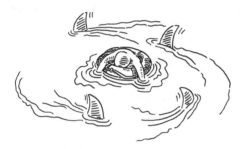

There are two schools of thought on how to persuade people to accept and support a change program. One is to sell the benefits of changing, and the other is to highlight the consequences of not changing. Research suggests that people are more influenced by negative consequences than positive ones, but we'll leave that to the sociologists to debate.[17]

In his article "Leading Change: Why Transformation Efforts Fail," John P. Kotter wrote, "Employees will not make sacrifices, even if they are unhappy with the status quo, unless they believe that useful

---

17   K. Goldsmith and R. Dhar, "Negativity Bias and Task Motivation: Testing the Effectiveness of Positively versus Negatively Framed Incentives," *Journal of Experimental Psychology: Applied* 19, no. 4 (2013): 358–66, doi:10.1037/a0034415.

change is possible. Without credible communication, and a lot of it, the hearts and minds of the troops are never captured."[18]

If Kotter's right, the real question is, How do you define useful change? Clearly, organizations embark on change programs to benefit the organization. But improvement programs are also a significant investment in the working environment, and people are a key part of that. Many of the intended outcomes have benefits to individuals, not just to the organization.

So it comes down to crafting the message.

People listen to corporate messages from their own viewpoint and translate the message into how it will impact them personally. There's an expression that most managers are familiar with—"What's in it for me?"—or WIIFM, as it's usually written on management training posters.

"What's in it for me?" implies that people naturally have their own best interests in mind. When you're trying to sell them on the virtues of changing what they do, you must articulate why the change will be better for them.

But there's another Latin expression, "Cui bono?" Attributed to Cicero, the expression means "To whose benefit?" In a legal context, it insinuates that the guilty party can usually be found among the individuals who have something to gain from the crime.

"What's in it for me?" is similar, but it is not the same as "To whose benefit?" "What's in it for me?" is asked by individuals trying to determine whether the changes will make them better off personally. "To whose benefit?" is asked by individuals trying to figure out who

---

the changes are really going to benefit. Sometimes employees suspect that the benefit may be mostly to the company and not to themselves.

WHY SELLING ASPIRINS, NOT VITAMINS, IS MORE EFFECTIVE

It's hard to get people to change their behavior by trying to sell them on the notion that the company will become more profitable as a result. It's also hard to convince them that the reason for change is to 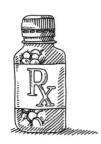 benefit them as individuals. But somewhere between those extremes is a believable argument.

To change behavior patterns, one approach is for senior leaders to convince people that the change will fix specific "pains." Dan and Chip Heath, the authors of *Made to Stick: Why Some Ideas Survive and Others Die*, wrote, "If entrepreneurs want to succeed, as venture capitalists like to say, they'd better be selling aspirin rather than vitamins. Vitamins are nice; they're healthy. But aspirin cures your pain; it's not a nice-to-have, it's a must-have."[19]

Executives can do this by translating the organization's vision into how changes will improve the current environment for their people. The results equation is a helpful framework to do that. For example, improving processes reduces daily frustrations. It gives managers the tools and training to improve their ability to support their staff more effectively. Performance improvement creates job security and promotes career advancement.

---

19   Chip Heath and Dan Heath, *Made to Stick: Why Some Ideas Survive and Others Die* (New York: Random House, 2007).

AN EFFECTIVE WAY TO PRESENT COMPLEX CHANGE

We do these presentations on large wall maps. The large wall maps visually illustrate the connections among what you're going to change (the process), how you're going to manage these new processes (the performance systems), and what you need to physically do differently (people's behaviors and skills).

Every so often we get asked about the wall maps and why we don't simply project the presentations in a more typical slideshow format. While useful for many things, the problem with slideshows is that once a slide is presented, it disappears.

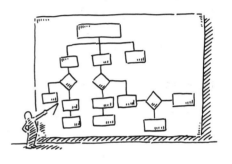

Then another slide is presented, and it too disappears. After a few slides, people forget what was presented beforehand, and the continuity of the message disappears.

The real power of the wall map is that it keeps all the key points front and center, and people can easily scan back to review previous points. This allows them to make the connections that are often important to fully understand how you get from A to B.

Another benefit of using wall maps is that it stops the endless internal debate of whether to hand out a slide deck before the presentation. If you hand it out, people tend to jump ahead and pay less attention to what's being presented. If you don't hand it out, people feel that you're withholding information.

Although it's now usually a digital file rather than a physical document, similar issues remain. With the wall map, everything is in full view. You just need to explain it.

AVOID THE TRAPS

Regardless of whether the vision plays off the positives of change or the negatives of not changing, there are a few traps to avoid.

MAKE SURE PEOPLE UNDERSTAND THE MESSAGE

What you say and what people hear are not always the same thing. People don't always ask for clarity, even when they aren't entirely sure what's been said. We see this in our own company. People are often uncomfortable asking questions in groups for fear that they *should* know the answer. Social styles, organizational dynamics, upbringing, and cultural norms can all get in the way.

Because we travel to our clients' locations, it's often difficult to get all our staff together in one place at one time. Twice a year we try to bring everybody under one roof somewhere so that we can communicate company strategies and results.

What you say and what people hear are not always the same thing.

We have an open meeting, where our executives discuss the results and plans of the various parts of the business. The functional plans, as is the case with many organizations, often introduce changes of one kind or another. During the actual meeting, there are rarely any questions asked, which sometimes fools us into thinking the message was clear and well communicated.

With surprising frequency, the next day we find that there's been a disconnect somewhere between what was intended in the messaging and what our employees took away from it.

At one meeting, myself and a few others spent some hours going through details about our positioning, performance, and people strategies. Despite the amount of information provided, all that people remembered is when I said, "The core of our people strategy this year is to improve our recruiting."

What I meant, of course, was that people are critical to a consulting firm, and it's a good idea to improve how you try to attract the best candidates. What people heard was this: "We need to improve the quality of our people," meaning: "Find better staff than all of you here."

It caused a surprising amount of internal turmoil. It also caused other key points from the meeting to be lost. It was an innocent comment, but when your job is to communicate ideas, which is a key responsibility of all leaders and managers, it is important that what you say and what people hear are the same thing.

To minimize the chance of a disconnect between message and understanding, leaders should debrief after a meeting with smaller groups to probe what was communicated or missed. In these meetings the leaders should ask the questions rather than ask *for* questions. If there are significant misinterpretations, a series of postbriefings should be rolled out, again with smaller groups, to ensure that the appropriate message is carried forward.

FORGET THE PLATITUDE TO WORK SMARTER, NOT HARDER

Some organizations try to wrap their change program under the banner of "Work Smarter, Not Harder." It's not a great rallying cry for change. The expression subtly implies that you can get something for nothing. Change is never easy, and not all changes are win-win.

People can become cynical if a change is oversold. Sometimes working smarter does mean working harder. It certainly means you're working differently. Something must be given up in exchange for something else that is hopefully better.

If you streamline a process by removing recurring daily obstacles, it can be misleading to suggest that working harder isn't a possible outcome. If a process constantly breaks down, leaving a person with little to do, fixing the problem may result in that person working more.

However, most people we observe have no objection to putting in a fair day's work for a fair day's pay; it's the recurring problems that frustrate them and that make work tedious. Fixing those problems creates a better environment and that's what needs to be marketed. Leaders must explain why the net balance is better, recognizing the losses as well as the gains.

"Working smarter" for a manager often means becoming more involved in the scheduling of work and following up on the process. It usually means a more focused diligence is required. At least initially, managers may find these new requirements "harder" because they aren't familiar with them and because they change their patterns of behavior.

The objective is to enhance the organization's performance, but it's important to acknowledge the effort required to achieve this goal. However, it's also essential to communicate the benefits of improved management to individuals.

APPRECIATE CULTURAL CONTEXT

For several years, we conducted a training session about problem-solving that used an interesting deception. In it, we presented a paragraph that describes a young charismatic leader of a nation facing a tough decision.

> The new chief executive, one of the youngest in his nation's history, is being sworn into office on a bleak, cold, cloudy day in January. Standing beside him is his predecessor, a military leader who had led the nation through a world war. The new chief executive was raised as a Catholic and rose to his new position in part because of his vibrant charisma. He is revered by the people and will play a crucial role in a military crisis that will face his nation. His name will become legendary.[20]

Participants were asked to guess who we were describing. Given the historical and personal details, it was easy to conclude that it was John F. Kennedy, which pretty much everyone figured out halfway through the exercise. The plot twist is that the correct answer is not John F. Kennedy—it's Adolf Hitler. The exercise was designed to demonstrate people's natural tendency to jump to conclusions too quickly and to exclude alternatives.

---

20   Morgan D. Jones, *The Thinker's Toolkit: 14 Powerful Techniques for Problem Solving* (New York: Rev, 1998), 40.

The exercise demonstrated this point brilliantly every time we used it, except once. We were doing some work in Europe, and the company asked us to train some of their quality managers in Istanbul. The session was going well, then we got to the problem-solving exercise.

 A slide came up asking, "Who is the person in the following riddle?" The answer it provoked is remembered as one of the more confusing moments in the history of Carpedia training.

While we waited, anticipating the usual wrong answer, the quality managers looked at one another a little awkwardly and said, virtually in unison, "That sounds like Adolf Hitler."

There were a few additional grumblings about whether Adolf Hitler was an appropriate leader to showcase. Not a single person saw the description as one of John F. Kennedy, even after it was explained how the exercise was supposed to play out.

Companies are full of individuals from different backgrounds, religions, cultures, and ideologies. Sometimes it's easy to forget how the message gets translated. Humor and clever anecdotes are also understood based on cultural context and should be avoided in multicultural environments unless properly vetted in advance.

MANAGE THE HEADLINES

Although we suggested limiting the number of new concepts introduced in a meeting to avoid confusing people, like all seemingly good advice, there's a caveat. You also need to manage the headlines.

The expression comes from how news organizations throw a summary headline onto the top of a story to create a short, catchy sound bite. These headlines are what people remember and what they tend to repeat to others afterward.

A top client gave us this advice as we were preparing to present to the board members some studies we'd done on their sales organization. We had just shown him that the aggregate amount of time their sales reps were actively selling was only about 10 percent of the available time.

He simply said, "You need to manage that headline. If that's the only thing people take away from the meeting, it will be very difficult to get the sales group on board."

He was right. Although the studies were accurate, they didn't tell the whole story. The salespeople also spent about 20 percent of their time with clients developing relationships, which was also important. If we isolated the fact that only 10 percent of the time was actively  selling, that headline alone would be not only uncomplimentary but also unfair to the sales team.

One of the more infamous examples of this happened in May 2003, just off the California coast. Former President George W. Bush, aboard the aircraft carrier USS *Abraham Lincoln*, declared that "major combat operations in Iraq have ended" under a large "Mission Accomplished" banner.

By the time US combat operations in Iraq were finally halted, eight years later, more than three thousand additional American military personnel had lost their lives. Although Mr. Bush never actually said "mission accomplished" in his speech, the banner was the only thing people remember from it.[21]

DON'T GIVE MIXED MESSAGES

Messaging needs to align throughout the organization. What senior leaders say gets rolled down to the frontline employees. Employees often trust their immediate manager more than they do senior executives, and so the words and actions of their manager are very important.

What frontline management says can either communicate alignment or cause confusion. Management credibility is damaged if the message wavers, seems uncertain, or contradicts what others say.

Managers must avoid saying things like, "We're going to give this new way a try and see if it works," or "We're just testing this new system; don't worry, nothing's carved in stone." This is an easy trap to fall into because it's comfortable, but it lets everyone off the hook, the manager included.

For change to stick, people need to understand that the status quo is not an option.

Leaders and managers also need to anticipate questions and concerns that employees may have so that they can develop a consistent and genuine response. One of the areas that can get managers into trouble is how they handle questions about reducing labor costs.

In early communications, managers will be confronted with a question about how this initiative will impact people's work hours or jobs. How those questions are handled can severely harm employee engagement.

Some organizations have clear policies on attrition that help clarify the response. In other cases, managers really don't know at an early stage what the potential outcomes might be, and stating that sincerely is far more effective than guessing.

For change to stick, people need to understand that the status quo is not an option.

WHERE TO LOOK

The Results Equation

Assess the Opportunity

Create a Results Strategy

WHAT TO IMPROVE

Improve Processes

Align Performance

Develop People

HOW TO GET RESULTS

Focus the Effort

PREPARE FOR CHANGE

Implement Change

Mindset Principle: Walk the Track

The Prepare for Change phase is designed to get the system tools ready and to prepare management prior to a full implementation. There are two main aspects: training managers and prototyping method changes.

Organize for Change
- Know what to expect
- Develop countdown schedules

Train and Coach Managers
- Training overview
- Social styles and management styles
- Planning
- Communicating
- Following up
- Problem-solving

Conduct Prototypes
- How to set up a prototype
- Process considerations
- Performance system considerations
- People considerations

PREPARE FOR CHANGE

Every battle is won before it is ever fought.

—SUN TZU

We took a high-speed driving course on an old Formula 1 racetrack just outside of Montreal. I went with the other founder of Carpedia, Greg Tremblay, and my two brothers, Toby and Mark. Toby was the best driver and liked to remind us of it. He decided to make a point of it on the second day by needlessly driving Greg off the road.

A funny thing happened. The conversation over dinner that night wasn't about my brother's reckless driving or about how exciting it was to drive open-wheel  race cars—it was about how good the actual training program was. Maybe that said something about us.

In a nutshell, the instructors broke down high-speed racing into two things: driving in a straight line and driving around corners. To be a good driver, you had to master these two skills. They further broke down each of these two skills into specific steps. For example, driving around corners consisted of braking in a straight line, turning at a steady speed to the apex, then accelerating to the corner exit. Some of these skills were counterintuitive.

They would teach one skill in the classroom and then take us out to the track to practice. Gradually we learned how to combine the various skills. Athletic coaches use a similar technique to teach athletes where to position themselves and what to do while their often-chaotic environment swirls around them.

The driving course left an indelible impression and made us go back and change the way we prepare managers for implementation. We broke down manager skills into base components, assigning work, following up, and problem-solving, for example. We developed an approach that allowed them to practice these elements in isolation before combining them in the general whirlwind of the real world. It made us better integrate the interplay among process management, effectively using performance system tools, and interacting with employees.

I'm not sure that we've ever achieved the clarity of the original training course, but it gave us a more logical and practical approach to getting managers prepared for change.

ORGANIZE FOR CHANGE

No matter how prepared you think you are, it's always a good idea to think through what can go wrong. Following that initial driving course, we decided to test our skills at the Mosport International

Raceway, since renamed the Canadian Tire Motorsport Park.[22] Located in an unassuming rural town named Bowmanville, northeast of Toronto, the track is considered to be very challenging and has had many Formula 1 world champions race around it.

Despite this daunting pedigree, each spring and fall for about ten years, a few of our braver employees put their cars and themselves at risk to test their driving skills.

KNOW WHAT TO EXPECT

At each event, a professional driver would take part to coach and train as needed. And every year, first thing in the morning, he made everyone walk the track before anyone was allowed to race.

Every year all participants would drive their cars toward the first turn, walk the curve, and then go back to their cars and head to the next corner. Every year people would complain about the repetition and the amount of time it took, and every year, by the end of the day, everyone was grateful for being reminded of how important it was to walk the track.

The professional driver had raced all over the world in many types of cars and had raced around the Mosport track thousands of times. Yet when he walked around the track and explained the correct driving techniques and the associated dangers of the turn and angles in the road, he did so with a deep respect for the track.

Sure enough, sometime during the day, typically after lunch when people started to fatigue, someone would lose focus for just one moment and learn firsthand why that respect was important. At very high speeds, everything is magnified: the steering, the braking,

---

22   "Canadian Tire Motorsport Park," Wikipedia, last modified March 25, 2023, https://en.wikipedia.org/wiki/Canadian_Tire_Motorsport_Park#History.

the balance of the car's weight. When you make a mistake at high speed, things can turn badly very quickly.

When you're driving at high speed, you also don't fully appreciate how much of the track you cover very quickly. Watching the road directly in front of the car, rather than up ahead to the next corner, is an easy habit to fall into.

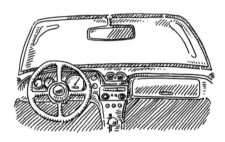

When you have a professional driver to coach you around the track, one of the things you can't help but notice is how often the person will tell you, "Get your eyes up. Look where you want to go, not where you're going."

The reason, instructors explain, is that your body and your brain work in a coordinated manner, and the car will go where your eyes are looking. So if you're going around a corner at high speed and a wall is approaching, you need to avoid fixating on the wall, or you'll tend to drive toward it rather than away from it. You need to keep your eyes well ahead and trust that the car will follow where you're looking.

My older brother, the better driver, learned this lesson one sunny afternoon. He took a corner slightly wide and let the back wheels get off the road. The car spun around and shot him across the track into a retaining wall. Fortunately, he was fine, although his car and his ego were a little banged up.

Greg later claimed it was karma for the training incident.

We try to apply this same thinking with change programs. When you're navigating change in an organization, there are many walls to avoid. You can't eliminate them, but you can manage around them by knowing where they are, knowing the course and staying committed to it, and staying focused on where you want to go. You can also have a contingency plan in case the wheels go off the road.

The Focus Meeting provided the basic game plan for what changes will be implemented. It identified the roll-out plan by functional areas, locations or regions, and the responsible operating leaders and managers.

But following the Focus Meeting, there are still several things that need to happen to properly prepare managers and employees for implementation. Three ways we do this are to develop countdown schedules, conduct formal training sessions, and prototype a few targeted areas.

DEVELOP COUNTDOWN SCHEDULES

One of the ways we avoid driving into walls is by building countdown schedules. Each key work stream needs a tailored plan identifying the nuts and bolts of the actual change migration.

This includes performance planning, resource requirements, technology changes, management and skills training, and other related activities. Often multiple changes are occurring simultaneously, so the road map also needs to address interfunctional dependencies and an appropriate critical path.

The countdown schedule is the final preparation for whatever area is being changed, so it needs to be tightly managed. All aspects must be completed to make sure the operating area is ready and prepared to go live with new methods. All the required system tools must be created and tested with real data, and all managers must be trained and comfortable with each tool and how it is to be used.

The initial project schedule is intentionally broad in its description of activities. But by this point in the initiative, there are very specific things that need to happen prior to going live. This includes changing the layout of an area, refining digital tools, or modifying supplier delivery patterns. All these things take some time and coordination, so they need to be identified and sequenced with whomever needs to be involved.

Countdown schedules need to be developed with senior area leaders to ensure they are responsible for deliverables. Most of the work required should be assigned to and completed by the operating personnel. The schedules should be reviewed daily (or at an appropriate cadence) to make sure everything stays on track. When some things go off track, which they are prone to do, you need to develop an action plan to get them back on track.

One benefit of countdown schedules is that it gives the change agent an opportunity to see the social style and planning skills of the area manager. This can be helpful in anticipating what to expect in the broader implementation.

TRAIN AND COACH MANAGERS

A common problem with many management training programs is that they overload managers with slides that tell them, in technical terms, what they should do and what to expect. They rarely break down management skills and get managers to practice those skills in pieces before trying to put them all together.

One of the results is that many managers know *what* to do, but they don't always know *how* to do it.

For management training to be effective and useful, concepts need to be deconstructed and practiced in the environment of the manager. We try to do this in two ways. First, we conduct training sessions that explain the purpose and intent of the performance system tools and how to use them to interact with employees.

The second approach is through a process called prototyping, where we get the managers to practice using new tools and new behaviors in a controlled environment.

TRAINING OVERVIEW

We've discussed the importance of management in a high-performance organization and the necessity to provide managers with the tools and environment they need to be successful. By this point, planning, execution, and reporting tools will have been either refined or developed.

The training sessions allow managers to practice using the tools and teach them how to effectively engage with their employees.

Often these sessions spend time making sure managers understand how daily or weekly work plans align to the overall expectations of the organization. As we mentioned in the assessment phase, senior executives deal with financial data, senior managers deal with planning data, and frontline managers deal with execution data.

To align these different planning horizons, we'll do several exercises to help a manager understand what a budgeted financial number means in terms of scheduling activities for their team.

In chapter 6, we discussed many of the gaps between what most managers do and what ideally they could, or should, do. We also mentioned that managers, at least initially, don't necessarily see their current behavior as an issue. Joint management studies hopefully ready them for the training sessions by giving them a better understanding of their current behaviors.

The bulk of practical training is geared toward how managers interact with their employees. If a manager's primary job is to remove obstacles that impede the effectiveness of their employees, they must be able to engage in a helpful, positive way.

If the performance system is properly designed, it should help managers identify where the obstacles are. What managers do with that information, and the behaviors they need to make the interaction effective, is the purpose of the training sessions.

SOCIAL STYLES AND MANAGEMENT STYLES

Part of getting managers to change behavior is understanding what type of person they are and what type of management style they have and in turn getting them to understand what type of people they're managing.

Social styles are a useful concept to help understand why people behave in certain ways and how they respond to certain situations. For managers, it helps to better understand how to communicate and interact with their employees and provides them with different techniques they can use to coach and motivate those people.

Several organizations have developed assessment tools that provide insights linking personal style and behavior. Myers-Briggs, Gallup's StrengthsFinder, and DiSC are some of the better-known assessments. We've tried a few of them and found that most of the personality categorizations are variations on a similar theme. We use a framework called the Social Style Model developed by the Tracom Group.

At the risk of oversimplifying their model, it suggests that some people are assertive while others are passive; some are responsive while others are more reserved; there are various combinations of all of these. People can modify how they act for periods of time, but they will generally revert to their dominant style, particularly when they're under stress.

The model suggests different approaches that managers can use to be more effective with the type of individual they're trying to coach. This is helpful for interactions such as work assignment or following up. People with different social styles react differently to how questions are asked or how information is presented. The model provides a guide to what motivates people and what discourages them.

We differentiate between social styles and management styles. Social styles reflect an individual's approach, whereas management styles tend to reflect the organizational culture. Some organizations have a more assertive style while others have a more passive approach. Some organizations have an autocratic management style while others are more consensus-driven.

The culture often reflects the nature of the senior leaders. On their way up through the ranks, executives often hire and promote people like themselves, which over time creates a certain corporate management style. It's one of the reasons why corporate mergers can be so difficult: two similar businesses can have very different management styles.

From a practical perspective, it's easier to modify specific management *behaviors* than it is to modify a person's social style or management style. Training sessions with managers focus on the behaviors that affect how they interact with their employees. Specifically, it focuses on the principles of dynamic management—on how managers plan assignments, communicate them, follow up, and problem solve.

DYNAMIC MANAGEMENT

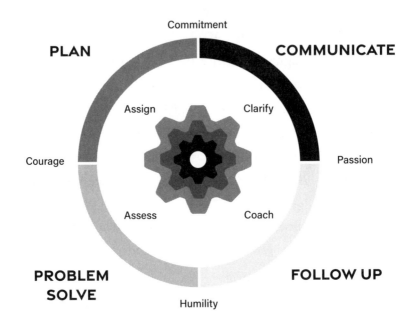

PLANNING

Planning effectively requires understanding how to use the planning tools of the performance system. Performance systems are designed to provide managers with a plan, but as we've discussed, they often lack critical elements. To help managers assign work more effectively, they need to take the appropriate time to review or prepare work plans. They need clarity on what they're trying to achieve, the specific tasks required, and the work processing time.

> It's easier to modify specific management *behaviors* than it is to modify a person's social style or management style.

If they're provided with a plan, or schedule, they need to understand the underlying parameters. They must be comfortable that the plan accurately reflects requirements and that it's attainable and realistic.

COMMUNICATING

When managers assign work, they need to make sure people properly understand what is expected of them. It's easy, and more comfortable, to omit or be vague about specific time requirements, but that's a key element of assignment.

While you may not be able to change the nature of people, you can coach them to use different communication styles suited to the situation. We bridge communication styles with people's social styles to ensure that what managers say and what employees hear are the same message.

How leaders and managers communicate with their teams has always been an important topic, but it has become even more complex with contemporary thinking about diversity, equity, and inclusion (DEI). We  spend time highlighting how communication needs to bring people together and unite them around a common purpose while still considering individual differences.

We also discuss how communication flows among levels of the organization and among functional areas. A lot of management communication occurs in meetings of various kinds. Managers are often not specifically trained in how to make meetings effective. The purpose and cadence of meetings, who should or shouldn't attend, agenda topics, and postmeeting expectations are typical areas we review.

FOLLOWING UP

Follow-up training focuses on purpose and content. You need to provide your team members support, but what intervals are appropriate to follow up? This topic requires clarifying the role of a manager, and that role can vary significantly by industry and function.

The content component is based on understanding the purpose of planning tools and how to use them effectively. Attainment of the plan is a mutual objective shared between the manager and the team member, but roles and expectations need to be defined. The communication skill we focus on for follow up is active listening. Active listening requires attention and diligence and goes well beyond simply hearing words. It's not an innate skill, and although it is easy in concept, it's hard to do well.

PROBLEM-SOLVING

Effective problem-solving is crucial for maintaining results and for continuous improvement. Although well-designed management systems provide targets and identify variances, they are essentially inactive. Managers play a critical role in interpreting performance information, identifying variances, and taking action to address them in order to drive change. Without the proactive involvement of managers, even the best management systems will fail to bring about meaningful improvement.

Without the proactive involvement of managers, even the best management systems will fail to bring about meaningful improvement.

To make problem-solving a useful tool for managers, it needs to relate directly to how they plan attainment and manage their key performance indicators. There are four basic performance indicators for any area of an organization: attainment, service, productivity, and quality (or yield). Other indicators can be important depending on the environment, such as safety, but these are the four typical ones. Problem-solving needs to provide managers with the critical thinking that is required if these indicators are off plan.

But if problem-solving is required, what is the most appropriate method for a manager to use? American psychologist Abraham Maslow, famous for his hierarchy of needs, is also  credited with the phrase "If all you have is a hammer, everything looks like a nail." There are many good problem-solving techniques, all requiring different skills and capabilities.

To help managers determine what technique to use, we categorize operating problems into the three elements of the results equation: process, performance, and people. In earlier chapters on these elements, we identified many common problems managers face. There are specific techniques to address each type of operating problem.

Understanding how and when to apply them equips the manager with a versatile toolkit.

CONDUCT PROTOTYPES

The first significant purchase made by the Carpedia partnership, about four months after starting the company, was a custom-made pool table. It wasn't purchased because we wanted to be hip or trendy, as became fashionable a few years later with the dot-com start-ups. It was because we really enjoyed playing pool.

Two years later, the pool table had only been used twice. So what went so terribly wrong?

 Two things conspired to ruin the vision of playing pool at the office late into the evening. The first was arguably inexcusable for a management consulting firm: the table didn't fit the space.

It turns out that pool tables require quite a lot of room, and the space earmarked for the table was not very big. This should have been picked up in the design phase but was somehow overlooked in the excitement of the purchase.

To use the table on one side, we had to use child-size pool cues, which significantly took away from the experience. This little planning error, by the people who originally crafted Carpedia's methodology, has been quietly buried in the company archives.

The second problem was not foreseen but made sense in hindsight. Hanging around to play pool at the office after a long day of work wasn't nearly as much fun as playing pool at a local bar, where there were people and noise and action (ignoring the fact that neither plan went over particularly well with our spouses).

One of the lessons we took away from this disappointing experience was the importance of thinking about the impact that method changes have on the environment. Process changes shift the dynamics of how people function and interact, sometimes more than you realize.

It was one of the reasons we introduced prototyping, so we can test a change and observe what happens in and around the process.

We used that insight as justification to write off the cost of a little-used pool table.

HOW TO SET UP A PROTOTYPE

To help managers take theoretical concepts and apply them to real-world conditions, we develop specific prototypes where they can practice their skills.

The prototype is an installation technique used to prepare managers and employees for understanding how the new operating environment will work and where they fit into it before the actual full-scale implementation.

A prototype is a concentrated focus on one aspect of the process, typically in a constraint area, where all the things talked about come together—planning effec-tively, efficient interaction between managers and employees, performance systems, and real-time feedback and problem-solving.

A prototype is a scaled-down and controlled model of the new operating world. It's typically done over one week. It gives managers and employees a practical test run of managing and interacting differently. It helps remove some of the fear and trepidation of what's been presented.

An example of a prototype could be increasing the throughput of a specific machine or group of machines where work is bottlenecking. Or it could be modifying the way patients are discharged from a hospital to free up beds, or introducing a new scheduling method so that equipment is better utilized in an imaging lab. Each of these examples is part of larger, more complicated issues, but as isolated examples they illustrate new ways of managing and reinforce that change can have a positive impact.

The advantage of the prototype is that it *always* yields some success. There are invariably bumps along the way, but when it is well orchestrated, the attention on one aspect of the process, the intense involvement of management, and the focused concentration virtually guarantee that the exercise will be successful. Typical results are as follows:

- Throughput is up between 20 to 50 percent.

- Quality is improved by 15 to 20 percent.

- Downtime is reduced by 50 percent.

There are often other less measurable but equally important practical outcomes. For senior managers, it involves them in the project, and they get to see the new management process in action. The exercise helps to reinforce the feasibility of the Results Strategy.

For area managers, it's a chance to shift their behaviors gradually and naturally, particularly regarding how they interact with staff. It gets them comfortable using new system elements in a controlled manner. It provides them with tools and coaching to properly plan and assign work. It allows them to practice following up on the plan and communicating differently with employees.

The prototype gives managers a chance to observe a process and to see challenges that impede their employees. A key to getting people to change what they're doing is to involve them in observing their own environment, regardless of how familiar with it they think they are. Observation can refresh their perspective and offer different insights into what solutions might be effective, even if they were attempted previously.

It also gives them the ability to take generic solutions and properly modify them to their own environment. When managers conduct observations, it adds visibility to previously unrecognized problems and identifies additional method changes that could be deployed.

For employees, the prototype sets the expectation that things are going to change. They get to see how performance information will be used to support them, not simply evaluate them. They see direct involvement and support from senior executives. They are listened to and engaged in the change process. Sometimes they will see challenges that have existed for years disappear during the week.

For the project team, the prototype helps with the design of the performance management system. You get to see what works and what doesn't or where information is lacking. It also zeros in on which management behaviors need additional training.

> When managers conduct observations, it adds visibility to previously unrecognized problems and identifies additional method changes that could be deployed.

Perhaps most importantly, it shifts ownership of improvement from the project team to the area manager.

Changes aren't necessarily sustainable at this point, but the improvements demonstrate to everyone that they aren't as frightening as anticipated and that this new way of managing can yield tangible benefits to all involved.

The successes help create excitement within the group and provide a preview of what could be achieved throughout the rest of the organization. This excitement helps to carry the organization through to the implementation phase.

PROCESS CONSIDERATIONS

The prototype needs to take place at the limiting constraint or a relatively important part of the process where results can be measured. It should be done in a highly visible area that is accessible by all levels of management. Ideally, it's an area with relatively consistent volume

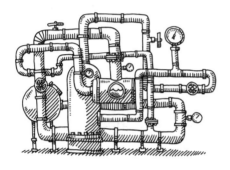

where method changes have been developed and can be tested.

If the prototyping involves machines, it's important to make sure that they've been properly maintained so that they don't break down in the middle of the exercise. Any required inputs should be prestaged or be adequately available. Other managers in adjacent departments that either feed information or parts to the process must ensure that those inputs are available and provided as required.

Process observations should be scheduled in advance, and managers should be trained so that they know how to do them. In product-based environments, it's helpful to have engineers or suppliers participate in both the planning and the debriefing of the prototype.

PERFORMANCE SYSTEM CONSIDERATIONS

As the point of the prototype is to achieve measurable results, it's important to have a clear baseline performance to measure against. The base period should reflect similar conditions to support a clear comparison. Key performance indicators should be derived from the base data if they're not already available.

The prototype demonstrates how an effective management system highlights challenges that occur during the process. Work plans, operating, and action item reports can all be developed or refined to identify performance, determine variances, or prompt actions needed.

Short daily meetings should be scheduled to review the results and observations, assign actions and method changes, and discuss communication problems with upstream and downstream areas.

PEOPLE CONSIDERATIONS

Involvement of the senior leaders is very important to ensure the success of the prototype. The executive team needs to cascade the purpose of the prototype and specific expectations down to the functional managers, then participate in a group meeting with all employees in the department.

Someone from the executive team should be involved, and ideally present, throughout the week to reinforce the importance of the initiative and to participate in daily performance reviews.

The area manager must ensure that daily plans are created the day before the scheduled activity. They need to practice communicating assignments and expectations in an organized daily huddle before the shift and to follow up on plan attainment at appropriate intervals. Performance from the previous day or shift should be reviewed and variances discussed with specific action items detailed.

The physical presence of a visual performance board can also support the manager when assigning work in the morning and holding performance reviews at the end of the shift. The board provides a clear-cut reason for

assigning work and following up on it. The board promotes behavior change by forcing the area manager to use the system elements.

To ensure ownership of the prototype, the project team should play a support role and let the area manager lead the prototype. The project team can help train and coach the area manager, as needed, throughout the prototype.

WHERE TO LOOK

The Results Equation

Assess the Opportunity

Create a Results Strategy

WHAT TO IMPROVE

Improve Processes

Align Performance

Develop People

HOW TO GET RESULTS

Focus the Effort

Prepare for Change

IMPLEMENT CHANGE

CHAPTER 9: IMPLEMENT CHANGE

Mindset Principle: Never Settle

Implementing change is part of an evolution in management capability; it's not an event. The objective is *not* to put a temporary focus on operations, make a few method changes, and claim victory. It's a transition to a new way to manage the organization.

Implementation Mindsets
- Care about results
- Don't quit
- Manage through momentum swings

Getting Results
- Leaders need to lead
- Managers need to manage
- Change agents support change

Cementing Your Gains
- Fix broken windows
- Build a high-performance culture
- The more you learn, the less you know

IMPLEMENT CHANGE

Execution is a specific set of behaviors and techniques that companies need to master in order to have competitive advantage.

—LARRY BOSSIDY

During the 1990s, violent crime in New York City dramatically declined. A number of theories have been suggested to help explain why this happened. One of the more interesting ones was the broken windows theory put forward by criminologists James Wilson and George Kelling.

They argued that if a broken window is left unrepaired, it suggests that people don't care about the condition of the building and invites others to do similar damage. So more windows will be broken.

Eventually the lack of respect and care will spread from the building to the surrounding environment and small crimes will lead to bigger crimes. As a

result, the city targeted controlling and minimizing relatively minor problems like panhandling and graffiti.[23]

There's been subsequent debate about causality and some of the assumptions of the original study. What we found most interesting about the theory is the impact the environment has and the importance of discipline.

The previous chapters have been written to help prepare an organization for change, but at some point you must make a leap from the relative safety of the way you currently do things to embrace a new way of doing things.

That's a big leap, and it is often where organizations stumble.

In this chapter we'll discuss what's needed to successfully implement change that sticks and the roles people play. We'll also cover some typical land mines you tend to encounter along the way.

IMPLEMENTATION MINDSETS

Implementation is about using new methods to operate and using new tools to manage performance. It's about modifying the behaviors of management *at all levels* of the organization. It's about creating an environment that allows managers to support their employees while continually looking to improve the performance of the organization.

Implementing change is hard work. It's the final heavy lifting required to get an organization to a higher performance level.

And it's the critical junction where good ideas and new behaviors either become the new way of doing things or they wither away as the gravitational pull of old habits takes hold. It takes courage to stay the course and to overcome the hurdles that inevitably surface.

---

23   Psychology Today Staff, "Broken Windows Theory," Psychology Today, accessed March 13, 2023, https://www.psychologytoday.com/ca/basics/broken-windows-theory.

Implementing change requires a few strong mindsets.

CARE ABOUT RESULTS

For permanent and lasting change, everyone involved needs to understand what's changing and to genuinely care about making those changes successful. Leaders must reinforce this by being very clear about what's important to the organization, and the people they manage need to share that understanding.

Broken windows of various sorts are common in most businesses, from obvious workflow clutter to performance boards that aren't kept up to date. They're often difficult to eradicate because, on their own, they aren't considered overly consequential.

But as the theory suggested, the lack of care for small things can have a ripple effect on others and may lead to a lack of attention to bigger, more important things. This lack of care is a mindset that needs to be addressed.

> For permanent and lasting change, everyone involved needs to understand what's changing and to genuinely care about making those changes successful.

The behaviors that result in broken windows reflect the mindset. The distinction between mindsets and behaviors matters because focusing on behavior alone may lead to temporary changes, but they won't be sustained.

We see this mindset problem frequently with a workplace organization methodology called 5S, often a component of manufacturing lean programs.

Although there are a few different ways to translate the original five Japanese words, in effect they are sort, systematize, shine, standardize, and self-discipline. The concept is sometimes thought of as a housekeeping method to make sure work areas are clean and well organized.

The real value of 5S is not its housekeeping aspect, although it's obviously good for that; it's that it engages employees at the front line to think about how work moves through their area. Employees can be a tremendous resource when they're engaged in their work. The 5S methodology provides them with a sense of control and makes problem-solving a daily activity. It's significantly more engaging than quality or service slogans.

The problem with 5S is that it's difficult to sustain. People need to believe it's important. It takes self-discipline and requires a mindset that supports and reinforces that discipline.

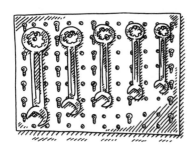

It's common for us to see 5S artifacts. In production plants, we often come across an artifact called a shadow board. Shadow boards are simple wall boards covered with what looks like chalk outlines designed to identify where things, such as tools, are supposed to go. They are both simple and practical and help people store and find what they need.

However, in practice, the outlines are often empty or filled with the wrong things in the wrong places.

So what causes these shadow boards to lose their appeal? Similar to linen closets or kitchen cupboards in people's homes, they require constant attention to remain organized. Everyone who uses them must be responsible and show care. As with broken windows, a lack of care can become a significant force over time. When shadow boards are empty, it reflects the mindset of the entire organization, shared by both managers and employees.

Unfortunately, 5S is often an example of how an implementation can go wrong.

DON'T QUIT

Quitting is another mindset that senior leaders need to consider before embarking on an implementation.

For most organizations, there will always be a portion of the workforce that doesn't want change to happen, or they want to quit at the first sign of obstacles and go back to how things were done before. Quitting is the easiest route.

These reactions can surface regardless of how well the purpose and benefits of the program have been communicated. Leaders need to anticipate this reaction and consider how they will manage the situation when it arises.

The Navy SEALs, the US Navy's famed special operations force, developed a recruiting process to make sure people don't quit in difficult situations. They put their new trainees in extraordinarily difficult situations and then *encourage* them to quit.

Their training program, called BUD/S (Basic Underwater Demolition/SEAL training), puts their highly qualified recruits through very demanding exercises, where the recruits are constantly reminded that they can "ring out" at any point, without judgment.

The majority who start the program don't finish it. When one ex-SEAL was asked what it takes to make it through the training, he replied, "It's simple. Don't quit."[24]

But the Navy SEALs' recruiting process is just that, a recruiting process. They've taken a page out of the Gallup organization's playbook by focusing on only selecting individuals who can demonstrate that they won't give up under *any* circumstances.

Most organizations don't operate under the same extreme conditions and don't have the same hiring practices. But implementing changes puts people in a position where they are frequently tempted to ring out. How leaders and managers handle these situations is very important.

When adversity surfaces, it's tempting to be apologetic and conciliatory or even to hedge commitment, but that never works. Employees need the security and reinforcement of strong, determined leadership. Managers must be visible and actively listen to their employees while at the same time reinforcing that the status quo is not an option.

MANAGE THROUGH MOMENTUM SWINGS

Visible leadership also can't be just symbolic.

Leaders can't show up for the kickoff event and then disappear. They need to remain visible and reinforce the company message for as long as it takes for methods and behaviors to take hold. Implementing change takes time, and success and failure comes in waves.

Positive and negative momentum swings happen in pretty much everything. You see it all the time in the economy with fluctuating

---

24   Paparelli, "It's Simple. Don't Quit," Paparelli.com, accessed March 13, 2023, https://www.paparelli.com/blog/life-advice-from-a-navy-seal.

stock markets, house prices, and inflation rates. You have good or bad streaks at the tables in casinos (at least until you run out of cash).

Similarly, implementations go through positive and negative momentum swings. Leaders of the organization need to support managers and workers through these periods.

Successful companies use positive momentum to their advantage and fight through negative swings. One of the reasons to demonstrate some quick wins early in an improvement initiative is to build some positive energy. The deliberate and careful staging of prototypes serves a similar purpose. The magnitude of the results is less important than the demonstration of improvement. These quick wins or successful trials give people the strength to believe that things can and will get better.

Most people are naturally more comfortable handling positive momentum. Negative momentum can do a lot of damage if you don't manage to turn it around.

But you don't need to tell that to Toronto Maple Leaf hockey fans.

Monday, May 13, 2013, will go down in sports folklore as one of the all-time incomprehensible chokes if you're a Leafs fan or as one of the all-time greatest comebacks if you're a Boston Bruins fan.

For nonhockey fans, the Leafs blew a 4 to 1 lead in the final period of the seventh and deciding playoff game. The Bruins scored halfway through the third period to make the score 4 to 2, then pulled their goalie with two minutes remaining. In those two minutes, they somehow managed to score two more goals to tie the game.

The Bruins went on to win the game in overtime.[25]

Pat Quinn, a former Toronto coach, described it as the terrifying moment that most athletes experience at some point in their careers: when momentum swings to the other team at such a fierce rate that the impending collapse actually becomes predictable. It's the awful moment when a coach looks at their team's bench and only sees players fearful that they'll be selected to go onto the ice.

Most people who watched this game shared this sense of impending doom (or elation, again depending on your perspective) well before the outcome of the game was determined.

If you've ever had the opportunity to play competitive team sports, you can appreciate how the players on both benches felt in that last period. You'd also know which team you'd rather be on. Some teams find a way to win. Some teams find a way to lose.

Unfortunately, negative momentum swings are pretty much inevitable, but they don't need to completely derail the implementation.

Staying with the sporting world for a moment, the 2022 FIFA World Cup final between Argentina and France was another

great example of significant momentum swings. Only this one showcased how two teams refused to buckle despite some dramatic positive and negative momentum swings.

25   Amalie Benjamin, "Game of the Decade: Bruins Stun Maple Leafs in Game 7 of 2013 First Round," NHL, January 19, 2020, https://www.nhl.com/news/game-of-the-decade-boston-stuns-toronto-game-7-2013-playoffs/c-313998466.

After being significantly outplayed in the first half, and with Argentina comfortably ahead by 2 to 0, France somehow shifted gears. With about ten minutes remaining in the match, France's Kylian Mbappé improbably scored two goals in two minutes to tie the game and send it into extra time.

Argentina was able to stop the momentum swing when legendary Lionel Messi scored his second goal to seemingly take back control of the game. Not to be outdone, Mbappé scored his third goal to tie the match once again.

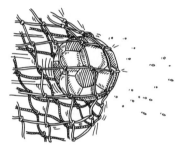

It eventually went to a penalty shoot-out where Argentina managed to pull out the victory.

In summarizing the game, journalist Cathal Kelly wrote, "How great was this match? So great that no one in it failed."[26] It was truly unfortunate that one of the teams had to lose, but it was a great example of where neither team allowed negative momentum to change their focus.

One of the ways to accept positive and negative momentum swings is to recognize that implementing change is part of an evolution in management capability; it's not an event. The objective is *not* to put a temporary focus on operations, make a few changes, and claim victory; it's a transition to a new way to manage the organization.

> Implementing change is part of an evolution in management capability; it's not an event.

---

26   Cathal Kelly, "World Cup Final Was One Perfect Game, a Truly Global Heritage Moment, in Which No One Failed," *The Globe and Mail*, December 18, 2022, https://www.theglobeandmail.com/sports/article-lionel-messi-argentina-wins.

In his book *Big Ideas to Big Results*, Robert H. Miles made this point when he wrote, "People in business have become so addicted to considering management interventions as events that they don't initially see a transformation effort as a permanent shift in the basic management process."[27]

Thinking of implementation as a transition rather than as an event gives it a more permanent orientation. It also allows for some scope for both positive and negative swings.

GETTING RESULTS

Implementing change takes strong leadership, but it also takes time.

When adapting to new work methodologies, organizations and individuals typically go through three phases: learning, understanding, and ownership. The first phase involves acquiring the knowledge of what to do and how to do it. The second phase involves discovering the reasons why these new practices are necessary. Finally, in the third

phase, individuals take full ownership of the new methods and start looking for ways to enhance and refine them.

The learning phase for a typical focus area takes three to six weeks. Managers and employees start to use the methods and tools that have been designed, but there is still some skepticism, and no one may have seen any tangible benefits yet.

---

27   Michael T. Kanazawa and Robert H. Miles, *Big Ideas to Big Results* (London: Pearson Education, 2015).

There is usually some resistance to change through this period, but the amount and duration rarely lasts more than a few weeks if leaders and managers remain committed and take appropriate action when necessary.

LEADERS NEED TO LEAD

Although leaders generally have a longer-term planning horizon, for the purposes of the learning phase, they have a heightened concentration on short-term planning and the specific key performance indicators (KPI) of the functional areas under them.

For the first few weeks, they review the daily operating report and discuss KPIs with their area managers. They know how their managers are reacting to volume fluctuations and whether the new methods are being used.

To keep a strong and consistent voice, leaders participate in an overall steering committee that meets weekly throughout the initiative. For simplicity and clarity, we keep weekly meetings to three agenda items: results, schedule, and people.

Results reviews the progress against key indicators; schedule reviews what has happened and what is being planned in the focus areas; and people is an open discussion of any communication, participation, or support requirements from those involved, directly or indirectly, with the work stream.

The individual work streams meet weekly with a similar agenda, chaired by the responsible area manager. For any work streams that leaders are involved with, they follow up on the specific results that were presented in the Focus Meeting.

A difficult challenge for leaders is dealing with the concerns and apprehensions some of their managers have. Managers may have previously requested additional resources and now view change as an indictment of what they were doing. Some planned changes might be things they suggested before, and they now feel they'll no longer get credit for their idea.

Implementing new methods and behaviors also causes changes in the social dynamics of the workplace, which can make managers uncertain about how their employees will react.

Some managers may disagree with basic underlying concepts, despite what they may have said at the Focus Meeting. They may not believe in the revised planning standards being used to determine resources for their area. They may have concerns about whether they can rely on other departments or about how they'll be able to handle emergencies with less resources. They lack the confidence to use the new tools and skills effectively.

Some of these concerns are understandable. Improving performance almost always means doing more with fewer resources, so operating problems become more obvious. There's less of a buffer to cushion the impact. It's like piloting a boat across a lake when suddenly someone lowers the water levels. The more you lower the level, the more you expose the rocks. The rocks are the operating challenges that managers must navigate around.

Examples of this might be the realization that people within the area are not sufficiently cross-trained, or the work staging areas aren't sufficient, or inputs from adjacent departments don't arrive on time. There may be errors in the new reporting tools or confusion about how to integrate the new methods.

Besides the new challenges that arise, the process of change itself can bring to light preexisting issues that were previously overlooked.

This might include large backlogs of work that become more apparent or quality concerns that now require more attention.

Actual resistance from managers tends to manifest in either active or passive ways. Active resistance is more apparent and vocal, which can feel intimidating at first. However, the advantage is that it's out in the open, and you can confront it head-on. With active resistance, you know where the managers stand and what their objec-  tions are. This provides an opportunity to understand and address their concerns collaboratively.

If you can successfully address these issues, their outspoken nature may lead them to become equally supportive of the initiative. A manager who is initially the most outspoken opponent of a change program can end up its greatest champion.

Resistance is more dangerous when it's passive-aggressive. This is the resistance you get when managers claim to support an initiative but don't really want it to succeed and quietly undermine it.

Passive-aggressive managers create distance by referring to changes as something that the organization needs rather than something they need. They're reluctant to embrace new approaches and often fail to intervene when their employees ignore the changes. By adopting an I'm-too-busy approach, they avoid responsibility.

They sometimes use the changes as a scapegoat for both past and present problems. They may also express their doubts, objections, or resentment in front of their employees instead of privately in their office to demonstrate support for their team.

Resistance at the management level needs to be confronted by senior leaders directly and quickly. Some people prefer to avoid confrontation, hoping these problems will eventually resolve themselves. Unfortunately, they rarely do. The problems usually get worse over time as negative momentum builds.

Leaders need to step in and defuse these situations as they surface.

MANAGERS NEED TO MANAGE

The implementation phase should reflect the behaviors that were practiced in the prototype. Managers must have a clear work plan and a well-thought-out schedule for the day for all resources that need to be managed. The work plan should reflect specific goals that align to the overall performance objectives.

At this early stage, the manager must make sure that each step in the new process is performed correctly and completely. Those tasks include the following:

- Clearly communicate the schedule and work expectations (both service and productivity) to employees.

- Know performance attainment at regular periods throughout the day (or week, as appropriate).

- If the area is not on track, know why, and problem solve with employees to get back on track.

- Review performance each day with the appropriate leader and discuss the achievement of KPIs, or the reasons for missing them, and required action plans.

Although change initiatives happen over many months, for the operating people involved, the time passes very quickly. A lot of information and learning happens in a very short span of time, and all of it occurs amid the whirlwind of normal operating issues. Regular and consistent weekly meetings are critical to reinforce accountability and to keep the initiative on track.

Like managers, employees have their own concerns and apprehensions, and it's common to experience various degrees of resistance.

Change can create morale problems, and occasionally you experience open expressions of resentment. Employees may display a general lack of cooperation or disregard for the new methods. If coworkers have lost work hours or have been laid off due to the changes, people may express their feelings by deliberately slowing their work down or by refusing to work overtime, or absenteeism may increase.

Managers must address these situations with compassion and understanding, but they can't ignore them. The success that results from using new methods will eventually reinforce the behaviors the organization wants.

> The success that results from using new methods will eventually reinforce the behaviors the organization wants.

After a few weeks, employees will begin to recognize the benefits of the new approach. In turn, resistance will begin to diminish as they become more familiar with the new ways of operating and interacting.

CHANGE AGENTS SUPPORT CHANGE

The primary role of change agents, whether internal or external, is to coach and support managers through the implementation. There are many new things that the area manager is juggling, and having someone available to coach, support, and occasionally prod is helpful.

In the week leading up to the implementation, change agents make sure that the area manager has all the tools they need. For example, work schedules, schedule controls, operating reports, and visual feedback tools.

These days we work with more and more companies that have their own internal performance improvement (PI) groups who act as change agents. As a corporate function, they have to navigate some resistance from operating groups, similar to external consultants.

These groups are often the offspring of a process-oriented improvement methodology, initially set up to help implement a specific corporate program, like Lean Six Sigma. As a result, they usually have strong process skills, but they may lack experience dealing with performance systems and organizational behavior.

Change agents need to be more than just number analysts. They must work directly with managers, in the manager's environment, to coach and support them as managers adjust to new behaviors. They need to understand the practical barriers managers face. Working in their environment also allows them to carefully separate reality from perception and chronic issues from anecdotes.

At the end of each shift, the change agent critiques each performance system tool, as technical and practical issues often need to be worked out. The change agent can adjust the tools or methods as required.

CEMENTING YOUR GAINS

A successful implementation means that an area or operation has been through a significant change in the way the process flows, in the way managers use performance systems to control the process, and in the way they interact with their staff. Improved performance is quantified through a measurable impact on financial results for the area. But a common mistake is to get to this new higher level of performance and declare victory too soon.

Within six months, managers should know how to mechanically use the methods and understand why they're important, but they still may not fully own them. It can take another six months to internalize how everything fits together.

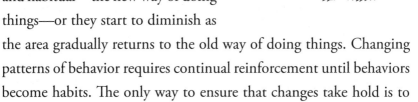

This period between understanding and owning is when changes either become embedded and habitual—the new way of doing things—or they start to diminish as the area gradually returns to the old way of doing things. Changing patterns of behavior requires continual reinforcement until behaviors become habits. The only way to ensure that changes take hold is to not allow regressions to occur.

Which brings us back to fixing broken windows.

FIX BROKEN WINDOWS

Broken windows, or red flags as we sometimes call them, are warning signs that the area or department is starting to return to former habits. These can seem relatively innocuous at first, but they collectively have a way of eroding performance gains over time.

Some process changes have the advantage of being all or nothing; for example, you might integrate robotic welding. As long as the machines work as planned, you have a good chance of keeping your improvements.

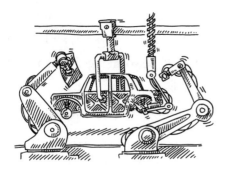

But many process changes are subtler. Examples could be method changes like increasing speeds on a line operation, or staggering shift starts, or upselling at the point of sale.

The broken window to watch for is lack of diligence, where line speeds start to return to prior levels, shift schedules become less staggered, or sales personnel stop attempting to upsell. These regressions are not always immediately apparent, as they tend to be gradual.

Often the deterioration manifests in a decline in operating performance. Process changes that rely on behavioral changes require continual monitoring and regular compliance reviews to ensure that they're sustained.

The performance system is an important tool for executives to manage improvement gains. But as we've discussed, budgets and operating plans quickly lose alignment if planning parameters disconnect from the business plan assumptions. This damages the integrity of all the underlying management tools.

This can happen when new activities change the business process but the planning standards aren't updated. When this occurs, managers stop using the resource plan to make resource decisions. Other broken windows include the following:

- Daily performance reviews don't have an agenda or become irregular or don't discuss specific performance by area and causes of variances.

- Visual performance charts aren't kept current or performance targets aren't accurate in operating reports and don't reflect the resource plan.

- New managers are hired or promoted. If they're not properly onboarded and don't know how to use the system, they can inadvertently cause or add to a slow decline.

But the most dangerous broken window is a systematic decline in accountability.

When an improvement initiative is underway, there's a heightened intensity and expectation that managers will change their behavior. When the focus on the initiative fades, there is a degree of relief at all levels, and some of the intensity naturally dissipates.

When organizations struggle to keep their gains, accountability is the thing that fades. You see this when plans are consistently missed and poor performance is rationalized. The fact that plans are missed isn't nearly as concerning as the rationalizing of poor performance.

The simple truth is that it's more difficult operating at higher performance levels. It requires more planning, more dynamic management, and more problem-solving. It takes perseverance to stay the course. Organizations that grow accustomed to accepting rationalizations without uncovering the root cause of variances have a difficult time performing at increasingly competitive levels.

The problem often starts in the middle. Frontline managers only maintain their new behaviors for as long as their area managers think it's important. If area managers don't hold them accountable to their numbers, they'll eventually stop managing by them.

Similarly, if senior leaders don't hold area managers accountable to their numbers, the accuracy of the information throughout the system deteriorates.

High-performance organizations don't let this happen. Although they may occasionally have flawed plans or make faulty assumptions, they proactively identify and rectify them before the next planning cycle.

BUILD A HIGH-PERFORMANCE CULTURE

Creating an aligned and accountable high-performance organization requires diligence for a period of six to eighteen months. Senior leaders, function leaders, managers, and change agents all play a role during this transitional period.

Senior leaders ensure that the financial and service objectives of the organization are clear to individual functions, and function leaders are held accountable for delivering against the targets.

Function leaders ensure that budget targets are aligned to the operating report targets. They use the performance system to identify variances to plans. Any changes or modifications to the performance system are approved by them and properly documented. New managers hired or promoted are properly trained.

Managers ensure that results are achieved and that each system element is used as designed. They use the performance system to identify off-plan conditions and to highlight the appropriate skills and their employees' need.

Change agents also play a role throughout this period. They conduct a quarterly review to assess process stability and the level of ownership of the installed management tools and method changes. They help monitor compliance of process and behavioral changes.

Within eighteen months, higher performance levels are fully owned by the operating managers. At this point the focus shifts to how to build on that improvement.

The initial assessment usually uncovers only about one-third of the potential improvement opportunities, leaving significant room for further growth. Senior leaders can leverage the performance system to identify the organizations' capacity and profit potential to drive growth and continue to elevate management capabilities. This is achieved by resetting the 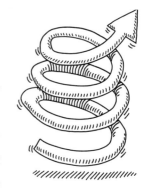 baseline performance through the budgeting process, which effectively reboots the improvement cycle.

Each year, prior to the budgeting process, a formal performance review should take place. Specific areas of the review include the following:

- A reconciliation of the improvement evaluation with actual financial performance

- Performance trends by key indicator

- A compilation of key initiatives, timing, progress, and impact

- An assessment of management alignment

As long as financial and operating indicators remain aligned through the budgeting process, leaders will have the appropriate visibility, and managers will have the appropriate accountability to continue to improve.

THE MORE YOU LEARN, THE LESS YOU KNOW

Alfred Whitehead, an English mathematician and philosopher, once said, "Knowledge shrinks as wisdom grows." There's a tendency in our industry to think we know quite a lot about the functional areas or businesses we study. Time and experience eventually teach us how much there is to learn and how little we actually know.

The most successful companies and executives we work for never lose sight of the gap between knowledge and wisdom. Despite their achievements, they remain remarkably humble and continue to discover new ways of doing things. Continual improvement can't be achieved without a genuine, unassuming willingness to learn.

We were working with a company that is a leading full-service nutrition bar and powder provider. They produce high volumes of nutrition bars of many shapes and sizes. The kind you find in the checkout lines at the local Starbucks.

You don't always think about it, but producing even something as common as a nutrition bar is a complex process. These bars come in various shapes and sizes, incorporating wafers and chocolate with fruits or nuts. They can be extruded, layered, coated, or drizzled with any number of creative combinations.

The base wafer is mixed in large batches and then gravity-fed onto wide conveyor lines, where it's flattened by a series of large metal rollers to a precise thickness. At different points along the line, the wafer is slit, layered with melted chocolate, mixed with toppings, cooled, and cut, all at constant speeds. Then it's sorted, sealed, wrapped, packaged, then stored or shipped to destinations all over the continent.

But it wasn't always that way. As the company grew, volume demands shaped and shifted the process so that more could be produced, faster and at less cost. The company brought us in to assist them when the volume demanded that they transition to a much more automated process.

Consider the dramatic shift in both mindsets and skill sets when this type of transition happens. Almost overnight, managers went from monitoring product inspection and packaging methods to optimizing the speed and uptime of highly automated machinery. The workforce makeup shifted.

Managers moved from coaching and interacting with skilled line workers to coaching and interacting with engineers and technicians. The requirement for different types of management information also shifted, as the organization's focus transitioned from labor productivity to equipment utilization.

Organizations can never stop adapting and never stop learning. Every evolution has an impact on processes, the performance systems required to manage them, and the skills and tools needed by the workforce.

The results equation provides a framework to help you manage these shifts as they occur.

The aim of this book is to simplify a complex methodology and to outline its fundamental principles. It is a compilation of the valuable lessons we have gained from our clients, mentors, and partners.

Our collective experiences will hopefully provide you with practical insights to navigate any challenges you may face and assist you in creating an exceptional organization.

ACKNOWLEDGMENTS

B eing truly innovative is a challenging task. In the early days of our company, my colleague Greg Tremblay and I would come up with creative ideas and become excited about their potential impact on business thought leadership. Almost inevitably we would discover that the same ideas had already been explored by others, or clients would patiently explain to us where the idea originated.

We gradually embraced the notion that our role was to aggregate good ideas. The concepts presented in this book are the culmination of years of learning from numerous mentors and clients as well as collaborating with Carpedia partners. We've had the privilege of working with many successful organizations and exceptional leaders whose contributions have significantly influenced our methods. Their insights and perspectives are reflected throughout the pages of this book.

There were a number of people within the company who helped shape the book with their thoughts and suggestions, mostly solicited.

Thank you, Greg Tremblay. The book, or the company, wouldn't be possible without your knowledge and insights over many years. Thank you also to Dan Lee. You've been a steady driving force for over twenty years. Your leadership and desire to make the firm a company of experiences continues to forge the culture of the organization.

Thank you also to my partners Jennie Link, Jordan de Lima, Sladjan Radic, Betty Warchol, Emma Bambrick, Andrew Rush, Jeff Janisse, and Bill McGinley for taking the time to read through draft chapters and adding valuable input on what was working and what wasn't. I thought it might be difficult for you to critique a founding partner, but none of you seemed to struggle with that. The well-deserved shots helped significantly.

Thank you, Ben Follows. As an author yourself, your critiques may have caused a virtual rewrite, but they certainly helped. Thank you also to Marie Lépinay and Sarran Bhola. Your input on illustrating concepts and reinforcing the important role of employees through the change process was very helpful.

I would also like to extend my sincere gratitude to all my current and past colleagues and partners who helped build the company into what it is today and without whom the book would have been very short. Although some of you have moved on to other adventures, your collective influence and impact still lingers in the firm.

I'm also very grateful for the valuable testimonials that were kindly provided for the book. Thank you to Sam Glaetzer, Scott Nygaard, MD, Patrick Volz, Jim Harrison, Len Wolin, Marco Calabretta-Duval, Greg Secord, Dave Johnston, Jean Filion, Tom Hogan, Bruce Hodges, Tony Pucillo, Michael Zaccagnino, Christina Jenkins, MD, Dave Arnold, and Andrew Brenton.

Thank you to everyone from the Forbes team who helped make the process very enjoyable. Special thanks to Mindy Cordell, my ever-diligent member experience manager, who somehow kept everything moving in the right direction. Thank you as well to Mel Sellick, my terrific book coach. Your keen insights and suggestions significantly shaped the book. It was a genuine pleasure working with both of you.

Thanks also to Nate Best, Steven Janiak, Henry Clougherty, Max Coffey, Matthew Morse, Kerrie Ann Frey, and Megan Elger for your support.

Finally, thank you to my family for your loving support. Thank you, Ben, for your friendly but blunt honesty, and Dalton, for your ongoing creative inspiration. Thanks, Isabelle, for your encouragement and companionship and for having the patience to reread the same chapters many times.

PETER FOLLOWS is an accomplished business executive, entrepreneur, and author and cofounded Carpedia International with Greg Tremblay in 1994. Carpedia is a results-based management consulting firm that helps organizations achieve lasting improvements in performance and profitability.

As the CEO of Carpedia, Peter provides the firm's overall strategic direction and is actively involved in product/service development and market-focused initiatives. He has extensive expertise in strategy, supply chain management, and operational effectiveness. He has provided consulting services to organizations in diverse industries across North America and Europe and has served on the boards of public and private organizations. Peter is the author of several published articles and wrote the highly regarded "52" series, which outlines Carpedia's unique methodology, business principles, and insights.

In addition to his professional accomplishments, Peter draws from a wealth of experience in other high-performance environments. He played Division 1 hockey and lacrosse at Harvard and was a member of the Canadian Men's National Lacrosse Team.

He is the proud father of two sons and currently resides in Toronto.

ABOUT CARPEDIA INTERNATIONAL

CARPEDIA INTERNATIONAL is a global management consulting firm that specializes in helping high-performing executives achieve lasting improvements in performance and profitability.

Carpedia has a remarkable track record in large-scale improvement programs, assisting clients in reaching their improvement goals over 90 percent of the time. The company offers services across diverse sectors, including manufacturing, financial services, healthcare, hospitality, retail, and logistics.

Many highly successful organizations, including the Ritz-Carlton Hotel Company, H. J. Heinz, ADP, Constellation Brands, FedEx, LVMH, CRH/Oldcastle, John Deere, Blackstone, Delta Airlines, and Yale New Haven Hospital, are among the firm's extensive list of past clients.

Carpedia has a team of experienced consultants who use a data-driven approach and work closely with their clients' managers to help them achieve their performance goals. The firm's focus on operational excellence and continuous improvement has helped it earn a reputation as a trusted advisor to many businesses around the world.

Ninety-four percent of all Carpedia clients will recommend its services to other organizations.

For more information, please visit www.Carpedia.com.

Seeing improvement in our financial statements is terrific, but feeling the enthusiasm about change and hearing a common language when I walk through production or any of our labs is what I will remember the most about this engagement.
—Manufacturing client

What was also impressive about the experience of working with Carpedia is the cultural change that I saw in the executive team.
—Technology client

We have improved service, the patient's surgical experience, and the provider experience as well as process predictability. Thanks to the efforts of your team, we are now equipped to sustainably own our results.
—Healthcare client

I would recommend Carpedia to any company who really wants to change their culture and become more efficient. I think we achieved so much success with Carpedia because they dug in with us and learned as they went, working closely with our management team. Our team feels that they own the process, program, and the success, all because of how Carpedia approaches the process.
—Hospitality client